Therapy Games

Creative Ways to Turn
Popular Games Into
Activities That Build
Self-Esteem, Teamwork,
Communication Skills,
Anger Management,
Self-Discovery,
and Coping Skills

By Alanna Jones

Rec Room Publishing LLC

---

www.gamesforgroups.com

Copyright © 2013 Alanna Jones

Library of Congress Control Number: 2013905666
ISBN-13: 978-0-9662341-5-2

A special thanks to my friends Lisa LaFrance, Jess Kury, Rachel Portillo, Laura Rhodes, and Jen Youngerman for playing games with me and for your willingness to have fun and be yourselves.

Contents

Introduction

The fun, interactive games found in this book are unique variations of popular games that can be used to enhance the therapeutic experience. By using one game in a variety of different ways, value is added to each game you own. The amount of time needed to prepare for each group session is simplified by mostly using the supplies provided with the games, with the occasional paper and pen added. *Discussion Prompts* are also included with each activity to simplify the therapeutic application.

In addition to making changes to existing games, it is also simple to use almost any ordinary board game as a therapeutic activity without making *any* changes to the game at all. The game can be used as an object lesson that leads to a discussion and teachable moment based on what occurs when playing the game. The discussion that occurs after the game opens the door for the lesson to take place.

Game Selection

You will find various "board games" used in this book to create new *Therapy Games*. Some of these games have been around for years and are commonly found in the family game closet such as SCRABBLE, MONOPOLY, and the OPERATION game.

Other games haven't been around for very long but have grown quickly in popularity. Many of these newer "board games" require group members to engage with one another in conversation and are considered "party games." This type of game is very interactive and can often be played in teams and with larger groups. Examples of interactive games are APPLES TO APPLES, TABOO, and IMAGINIFF.

Some of the "board games" used in this book will be more familiar to those who work in a therapeutic setting. The UNGAME is a good example of a game commonly utilized by counselors to help people open up in a non-threatening environment.

Other games, such as jigsaw puzzles, decks of cards, dice, and foam balls, don't require a board, but just simple props. These game props are easy to acquire, versatile, and simple to use.

No matter which types of games you choose, you will be able to use the same game over and over again. With all the game variations found in this book, each activity will always be a fresh and new experience.

You will find anywhere from five to twelve creative new variations for each "board game" or game prop used in this book. If you already own a number of these games, you will be able to pick up this book, grab a game off the shelf, and be ready for group. If your game library is currently very small, there are several games utilized that can be purchased even if you have a small budget. You will find a majority of the games used in this book to be common, affordable, easy to use, and easy to find.

Group Assessments

Games are a powerful tool for making observations and assessments about an individual's behavior. By observing behaviors during a competitive, or even a non-competitive game, the group leader will be able to make assessments about social skills, communication skills, anger control, and the individual's level of self-esteem and confidence. Once an assessment has been made, it will become clear what topics the individuals in your group need to focus on. With this assessment in mind, you can use the *Objective* that is listed with each game to find the right games for your group.

Group Goals and Objective

When planning your group session, it's important to know the goals and objectives you have for your group. The objectives should be based on the outcomes you are hoping to achieve. If a goal is to create an atmosphere where individuals can share more openly, then the games that focus on self-discovery will be best. (A complete index of the issues each game addresses can be found in the back of the book, and each individual game comes with its own *Objective*.) If a goal is to work on social skills, then use games that address communication skills, teamwork, or anger management. Games that address coping skills are primarily focused on finding new and healthy ways to use one's extra time. Free time tends to be a time when negative behavior occurs and exploring ways to fill this time with healthy alternatives is important for those who need it. Self-esteem games are always beneficial in our society where we are often told what it is we need to do better as opposed to what our strengths and talents are.

Discussion Prompts

The group discussion that takes place after playing a game is an extremely important part of the process of turning a regular game into a therapeutic experience. Without a discussion, the game is just a fun group interaction. Without debriefing what occurred during the course of play, participants will walk away from the session without digging deeper into their individual behaviors. The discussion will also create an opportunity to talk about the object lesson the game was meant to reveal.

At the beginning of each chapter, there are *Discussion Prompts* that can be used with the "board game" that is the focus of that chapter. These questions can be used when simply playing the game as it is meant to be played (without making any changes to the rules).

You will also find a list of *Discussion Prompts* with each game variation found in this book. The type of questions you ask will depend on the therapeutic outcome you want to address during your session. Each group has its own personality and sometimes you won't know what lesson will come out of an activity until it is played. Sometimes the competition itself will lead to behaviors that can be addressed.

Competition

Many of the games in this book offer an element of competition. The leader of any game can create a positive competitive atmosphere, where having fun is more important than winning the game. The leader can also create a more intense environment where winning is the main focus. How the game is presented makes a difference in the competitive experience for all those involved.

Competition is a very real part of life. Competition for jobs, promotions, to get into certain schools, to make the team, etc., can lead to stress and disappointment or excitement and pride. Playing competitive games and learning how to deal with losing can be a great life lesson. It's equally important to learn how to be a gracious winner.

My Hopes for You and Your Group Members

The games in this book are meant to enhance the therapeutic experience for both the leader and the participants through the power of play. My hope is that you will view "ordinary" board games in a new light after using the variations in this book. Perhaps you will even invent some of your own unique activities using games you already have to create a new therapeutic experience for your group. I hope you find these games useful, entertaining, engaging, productive, and fun for all those involved!

JENGA

The JENGA game is an individual challenge as well as a game. The challenge is to be the one who doesn't make the tower collapse. It can be played with very little setup and is easy to explain to anyone who joins the group.

For the games in this chapter, you can play with one JENGA game. Using a marker, write the number 1, 2, 3, 4, or 5 on the bottom of each brick (there should be ten of each number with four blank bricks left over). Also put a star on one of the blank bricks. Not all of the games need these numbers. However, your game will be all ready to go if you do this to your game to start with.

Game Summary

JENGA is a set of wood bricks that are stacked with three bricks for each layer. Players take turns carefully removing one brick from the stack and placing it on the top of the growing tower. As pieces are moved from the lower layers to the top, the tower becomes increasingly unstable until eventually the tower falls.

Therapeutic Applications of the JENGA game

This game is often used in the therapeutic setting as a way of answering questions. The way it is most commonly used is for group members to take turns answering a question for each brick they successfully remove and place on the top. It can also be used as a discussion prompt for ways to deal with feelings of anxiety or of feeling like your life is falling apart.

Discussion Prompts: Dealing with anxiety

1. When it was your turn, did you feel any anxiety?
2. What symptoms does your body display when you feel anxious?
3. What situations do you find yourself in when you feel the most anxious?
4. What are some things you can do to calm yourself down when you feel anxious?

Discussion Prompts: Feeling like your life is falling apart

1. Do you ever feel like your life is like a JENGA game when it is very fragile and about to fall with the slightest wrong movement?
2. Do you ever feel like your life is like a JENGA game that has crumbled?
3. When you feel fragile or like your life has already fallen apart, what do you do to cope with the difficulty that comes with being in this state?
4. What can you do to put your life back together when you feel like this?
5. How can others help you put your life back together?

JENGA
Games

Bigger and Better

Objective
To compare how much harder a group will work together to accomplish a task when there is a reward at stake than when there is no reward. To compare stress levels in individuals when there is more pressure to perform a task.

Who
People who experience stress in an unhealthy manner who need to talk about ways to deal with the stress. People who are only willing to do work when there is a reward in place.

Group Size
2 to 8 is ideal (but the game can be played with larger numbers)

Materials
- JENGA Game
- Some type of prize for the group (bag of candy, stickers, or other tangible items they would like) or you can offer something such as extra free play time or a game of their choice.

Description
Play the JENGA game one time just "for fun" and don't say anything else to the group about the game. Count how many layers the group can build up before the tower falls. For the second round, offer the group a prize for each layer achieved that is higher than the first time they played. This can be a piece of candy for each level, extra minutes of free time, etc. Count the levels as they play and hand out the reward afterwards. For added excitement, you may stipulate that they owe you something (cleaning, exercise, etc.) if the tower topples at a shorter level than it did the first time.

Discussion Prompts

1. Were you more relaxed the first time you played this game or the second? Why?
2. Did you feel stress when the whole team was counting on you to be successful when it was your turn?
3. How does your body let you know you are feeling stress?
4. Is stress a good or a bad thing for you? Why?
5. Are you willing to try your hardest when there is no reward or do you always need a reason to do your best?
6. If you only do your best when there is a reward involved, how does this impact your life?

Three Strikes You're Out

Objective
To talk about the consequences that come when someone continues to wrong others or society.

Who
People who often find themselves in trouble with authority figures.

Group Size
3 to 5 is ideal (but the game can be played with larger numbers)

Materials
➲ The JENGA game with the numbers 1, 2, 3, 4, or 5 written on the bottom of each brick. There should be ten of each number with four blank bricks left over.

Description
Play the JENGA game by taking turns pulling out one brick at a time and placing it on the top of the game. When someone pulls out a brick with a "1" on the bottom, they do not place it on the top of the game but instead they keep it. Once someone has a "1" and they pull out a "2," then they must place the 1 on the top of the game and keep the 2. Then do the same the next time they pull out a 3. Any block with a 4 or 5 on it, or that is blank, goes back on top and is not kept.

Once someone reaches a 3, then they have three strikes against them. They must sit out the game, and they can only watch the rest of the team play the game after placing their brick on the top.

Discussion Prompts
1. If you were someone who struck out and had to watch, how did it feel to be on the outside looking in?
2. Can you relate to "striking out" in your own life?
3. Can you think of a situation where you only get a few chances before someone or society gives up on you?

4. How many chances do you get in life to mess up before you are "out"? What would you define as being "out"?
5. Do you have any strikes against you right now?
6. Can you take back what you have done?
7. Can you make right something you have done that was wrong?
8. How can you move on after you have strikes against you?

Variations

➲ When someone gets eliminated, they can reenter the game when someone else gets eliminated.

➲ Use bricks with blank, 4 or 5 on them where a 4=1 and a 5=2 and blank = 3.

➲ Play "Five Strikes You're Out," going from 1 to 5.

➲ If the tower topples, each person starts where they left off (i.e., if you were holding a 2 brick, you would start with 2 strikes for the next game).

Magic Block

Objective
To talk about the need for some people to always be searching for the one thing that they feel will make their life complete, which can sometimes cause people to miss out on the good things they already have in their life.

Who
People who are so focused on getting to the next level (more money, more drugs, becoming more popular, finding a boyfriend/girlfriend, etc.) that they miss out on what they already have.

Group Size
2 to 8 is ideal (but the game can be played with larger numbers)

Materials
➲ The JENGA game with one block that has a star or other symbol marked on the bottom side of the block.

Description
Play the JENGA game with one block marked with a star (or other symbol). Offer a prize to the group if they can find the magic block before the tower falls. This can be anything from a treat to extra minutes of free play time or allowing the person who finds the star to select the next game the group plays. However, if the tower falls before anyone can find the magic block, then the group has to complete a task (this can be anything from cleaning, to exercise, to singing a silly song).

Discussion Prompts

1. Were you focused primarily on finding the star or were you enjoying the process of playing the game?
2. Once the star was found, did you want to continue to play the game to see how high the tower would go, or to see who would knock it over, or was the fun over?
3. Have you ever been so focused on getting something in your life that once you achieved it you were left wondering what to do next?
4. Is it good to have things in your life that you are striving to find?
5. Are there some things you could be striving for that are negative?
6. What things are you always searching for in your life?
7. Do you ever miss out on things in your life because you are so focused on a goal that only the future seems to matter?
8. How can you achieve balance in your life when striving to reach a goal?

Share and Learn

Objective
To encourage group members to open up and share about themselves in a non-threatening environment.

Who
People who need some encouragement to open up and share about themselves.

Group Size
2 to 8 is ideal (but the game can be played with larger numbers).

Materials
⊃ The JENGA game with the numbers 1, 2, 3, 4, or 5 written on the bottom of each brick. There should be ten of each number with four blank bricks left over.

Description
The number found on the bottom of the brick you pull out determines what you must do. A list follows that can be used or make one that fits the needs of your group.

1. Tell the group something you have a talent for or consider yourself good at doing.
2. Give a compliment to another member of the group. (This can always be the person on their right, a person of their choice, or a person the leader selects.)
3. Share something you would like to change about your life.
4. Share a goal you have for your life with the group.
5. Share something you have always wanted to do but have never done. Tell why you haven't done this

Blank: Choose any of the five questions to answer.

Discussion Prompts

1. What did you learn about someone else in the group that you didn't already know?
2. Did you prefer to give a compliment to someone else or to share about yourself? Why?
3. Did you share any goals or aspirations you have for your future? If so, what can you do to make these things happen?

Variations

➲ When the pile tumbles, the person who made it fall has to answer all the questions. (If it appears that individuals want to do this and are purposeful about knocking the tower over, then have them select other group members to answer the questions.)
➲ When you pull a blank block, you can choose a member of the group who gets to ask you one question.

10, 20, 30, 40, 50

Objective

To play a game of chance and focus on how some people seem to be luckier in life than others. Also, to discuss feelings people have when they feel their life is "unfair."

Who

People who make excuses for why they can't move forward in life. People who place the blame on outside circumstances, rather than doing what they can to improve their own situation.

Group Size

2 to 8 is ideal

Materials

➲ The JENGA game with the numbers 1, 2, 3, 4, or 5 written on the bottom of each brick. There should be ten of each number with four blank bricks left over.

Description

Play the JENGA game by taking turns pulling out one brick at a time. When someone pulls out a brick, they do not place it on the top of the game but instead they keep it until it is their turn again. After the first round, each person should be holding one brick which they will place on top of the tower, prior to pulling their next brick (which they hang on to until their next turn).

When the tower topples, each person should be holding onto a brick that has a number on it (except for the person who toppled the tower who possibly may not have a brick). At this point, announce an exercise that the group must do (jumping jacks, sit-ups, running in place, etc.), and everyone that has a 1 must do 10 repetitions, 2 equals 20 repetitions, and so on. Or you can do something for a set amount of time (running in place for 10 seconds, 20 seconds, and so on). If anyone had a blank brick, they get a free pass. The person who knocked the tower over is assigned the number 6 if they didn't manage to pull out a brick before it fell.

Discussion Prompts

1. Did you feel that the amount of exercise you had to do was fair or unfair? Why?
2. Do you ever feel like in your own life you are in an unfair situation where you have to do more work than others? What are these situations for you?
3. Do you ever look at others who you know and think it is unfair that they don't have to work as hard for something as you do?
4. If you feel your life is unfair, what do you do about it? Do you complain or do you realize you just might need to work a little harder to get the same things that others have?
5. Are you willing to work harder if your life is unfair? Why or why not?

Variations

➲ Offer a prize for completing the exercises to give the group incentive to do them, rather than just telling them to do so. This will also emphasize the message of some people working harder for a reward.
➲ Focus the discussion on the advantages of getting more exercise than others get.

Question Pile On

Objective
To encourage group members to open up and share about themselves in a non-threatening environment.

Who
People who need some encouragement to open up and share about themselves.

Group Size
2 to 8 is ideal (but the game can be played with larger numbers)

Materials
➲ The JENGA game with the numbers 1, 2, 3, 4, or 5 written on the bottom of each brick. There should be ten of each number with four blank bricks left over.
➲ Paper and pen or pencil
➲ A copy of the three question lists

Description
   Create three different lists of questions (or use the list provided on the following page). The first list should be simple "get to know you" questions, the second list should contain more revealing questions, and the third list deeper questions. The brick that is pulled from the pile determines the question that must be answered. If a "1" is pulled, then the person who pulled it answers a question from the first list, or does the same for a "2" or "3." If a 4 is pulled, the person must write down a question on a sheet of paper. If a 5 is pulled, the person must answer a question from the list created by those who pulled a 4. (If a 5 is pulled before anyone pulls a 4, the person doesn't have to answer a question.) When a blank brick is pulled, the person who pulled the brick gets a free pass and doesn't have to answer a question (or they can answer a question from any of the lists).

Discussion Prompts

Use the *Question List* to encourage group discussion.

Variations

➲ Assign a question to bricks 4 and 5 by making a longer list.
➲ When a blank brick is pulled, the person can select someone else in the group to ask them a question.

Question List

1. Get to know you
1. What is your favorite place to go out to eat?
2. What is your favorite sport to play?
3. What is your favorite sport to watch?
4. What is your favorite holiday?
5. What is your favorite store to shop at?
6. What is your favorite book?
7. What is your favorite movie?
8. What is your favorite class in school?
9. What is your favorite place to go for vacation?
10. What is your favorite thing to do when you have free time at home?

2. Open up
1. What is a talent you have that you are proud of?
2. What is something you wish you were better at?
3. Name something you like about your personality.
4. Name something you like about your appearance.
5. Name a goal you have for your life right now.
6. Which family member in your immediate family are you closest too and why?
7. Which family member in your extended family are you closest too and why?
8. What team or group of people do you feel most a part of when you are with them?
9. What would your dream job be?
10. What accomplishment are you most proud of?

3. Going deeper

1. What was the last thing you shed tears over?
2. Should you be trusted by others? Why or why not?
3. Have you ever cheated on a test? Why or why not?
4. Who is the person in your life who understands you the most? Why?
5. What should you do to change the course your life is on right now? Or, is your life going in the right direction?
6. What questions that others ask you make you most uncomfortable?
7. Can your friends depend on you? Why or why not?
8. Describe a time when someone hurt your feelings.
9. Do you wish you had more friends than you do now? Why or why not?
10. Do you have anyone in your life you need to ask for forgiveness (you don't have to name the person)? If so, can you share with the group what you need to ask forgiveness for?

Reverse

Objective
To provide a non-threatening game to help people open up about what they feel is missing in their life. To help people discover what it is they need to do to fill the holes they have in their life.

Who
People who try to fill the voids in their life with unhealthy things and who need to find healthy alternatives to fill the voids they feel.

Group Size
4 to 8 is ideal

Materials
➲   The JENGA game

Description
Instead of setting up the JENGA game in the regular fashion, set it up with only the outside blocks (so each level is missing the middle block). The tower will end up taller but with the middle sections all open. Challenge the group to fill in the gaps by taking a brick from the top and fitting it into one of the empty spaces. The group members should take turns, and you can allow them to use two hands to do this (but only allow them to touch the level they are putting the brick back into to make it more challenging). To make it extra challenging, allow them to use only one hand.

Ask the group members to think about the things that might be missing in their life that they want to add in order to live a healthier life emotionally or physically. Each time someone takes a brick from the top, they should tell the group what it is they want to add to their lives. Once the tower is complete, allow the group to play regular JENGA for fun before the group discussion time.

Discussion Prompts

1. Do you ever feel like you crumble and fall apart like a JENGA game?
2. Do you ever feel like you have holes in your life?
3. Do you ever feel like there are things missing in your life?
4. If you have things that are missing in your life, what do you try to fill this void with that is unhealthy?
5. Do you spend more time trying to fill the holes in your life from the past or moving onward and upward?
6. What holes in your life do you need to heal and move on from?
7. How can you fill the holes in your life in meaningful and healthy ways?
8. When do you feel like you are complete and whole?

Team Tower

Objective
To recognize how we are all individuals who most often work as a part of a team (with our family, coworkers, teammates, schoolmates, etc.).

Who
Individuals who need to recognize things they may need to change about themselves in order to get along better when in a group situation.

Group Size
4 or more

Materials
- ➲ The JENGA game with the numbers 1, 2, 3, 4, or 5 written on the bottom of each brick. There should be ten of each number with four blank bricks left over. One of the blank bricks should have a star on it.
- ➲ Paper and pen for keeping score

Description
   Divide the group into two teams and play the JENGA game with individuals from each team alternating removing blocks and placing them on top of the stack. Each time a block is pulled and successfully placed on the top of the game, the team who pulled gets to add the number from the bottom of that block to their score. If the star block is pulled, then the team earns ten bonus points. The team member who causes the tower to fall earns negative five points for his or her team. The team with the most points at the end is declared the winner.

Discussion Prompts

1. Do you like to play this game as an individual or as a part of a team better? Why?
2. In your life, do you find yourself in situations where you have to work as a part of a team or as an individual more often?
3. Do you think you can contribute to a team even if you work as an individual (e.g., in your family setting)?
4. Do you ever truly only work as an individual, or are you always a part of some sort of group?
5. What qualities do you have that make you easy to work with?
6. What qualities do you have that might make you difficult to work with?
7. Is there anything you can do to improve your ability to work with others?
8. Why is it important to be able to work with others?

Taller and Deeper

Objective
To provide a non-threatening environment where people can ask each other questions.

Who
People who need some encouragement to open up and share about themselves.

Group Size
2 to 8 is ideal (but the game can be played with larger numbers)

Materials
- The JENGA game
- The UNGAME cards

Description
　　Play the JENGA game. Each time someone pulls out a brick and successfully places it on top, they get to answer one question from the "1" pile of The UNGAME cards. Once the group has added five layers to the top of the game, replace the "1" cards with the deeper questions in the "2" card pile from The UNGAME. The person who topples the tower has to answer the previous three questions.

Discussion Prompts
1. Did you enjoy having the chance to answer questions in front of the group? Why or why not?
2. How often do you get the opportunity to share about yourself with others?
3. What did you learn about a member of this group that you didn't know before?

4. How often do you take the time to ask your friends and family members deep questions?
5. Do you like it when someone asks you questions about yourself or does it make you uncomfortable? Why?

Variations

➲ Use the JENGA game with the numbers 1 through 5 on the blocks. Whenever an even number is pulled, the person draws a card from the "2" pile, and whenever an odd number is pulled, they answer from the "1" pile.

➲ Play a regular game of JENGA. However, whenever someone pulls a brick and successfully places it on top, they get the opportunity to ask another member of the group a question. Encourage the group to ask deeper questions as the game progresses.

THERAPY GAMES

THE UNGAME

The UNGAME is a popular game in the therapeutic setting. Designed to be uncompetitive, the game creates a simple way for people to answer questions found on the cards to help players get to know and understand one another. You'll find several ways to use the UNGAME cards in this section of the book to create a whole new game or activity.

Game Summary

The UNGAME isn't so much a game as it is a set of question cards with a game board. The board is used to determine if you draw a card, make a comment, or ask a question. For the purpose of the games in this book, The UNGAME Pocket Size is all you need. The Pocket Size game comes with two sets of question cards. Set "1" is filled with more lighthearted, "get to know you" type of questions. Set "2" contains questions that are deeper in nature with more serious topics. Each set in the Pocket version contains 70 cards, and there is a small number in the bottom lower-right-hand corner of each card (this number is used in some of the games found in this book). There are also 15-16 cards in each set that say "You may ask a player one question or comment on any subject you choose." For the game variations found in this book, those cards will not be needed. The Pocket Size games are less expensive and more portable than the board game and are geared towards different populations. Pocket Size games are available for Teens, Kids, All Ages, Seniors, Twenty Somethings, Families, Christians, and Couples. Each set is unique and offers appropriate questions for the group it is made for.

Therapeutic Applications of THE UNGAME

This game in itself has therapeutic value; it offers group members the chance to open up and answer questions in a non-threatening environment. Individuals should be given the choice to answer a question or not. If a group member chooses to pass on a question, the leader should determine if they can choose a new question or simply pass up their turn.

The Discussion Prompt questions in this section are often similar since the game itself will lead to a great opportunity for discussion. These questions can be used if you have people who seem to be reluctant to share during the course of the game. There's an opportunity to talk about listening skills as well. This game requires individuals to listen and not interrupt when someone else is sharing.

Discussion Prompts: Feelings about sharing openly
1. Did you enjoy having the opportunity to share about yourself?
2. Did you prefer the questions from the "1" pile or the "2" pile? Why?
3. Did you feel put on the spot when you were asked a question?
4. Do you get uncomfortable answering personal questions? Why or why not?

Discussion Prompts: Listening skills
1. How difficult is it to listen to someone else answering a question when you yourself want to be the one giving the answer?
2. Do you listen when others are sharing or are you thinking about what it is you want to be saying?
3. What did you learn about someone in the group that you didn't already know?

THE
UNGAME
Games

Down and Across

Objective
To create a non-threatening environment where individuals can answer questions and share more openly about themselves.

Who
Individuals who share more openly through the portal of a game than they would if simply asked a question.

Group Size
1 to 8 is ideal

Materials
➲ The UNGAME cards
➲ Pair of dice

Description
Using the cards that have a "1" on them (these are the lighthearted question cards), lay them out on a table in six by six rows, and face down. There should be six rows across and six down. For this activity omit the "Question or Comment" cards.

To play the game, group members take turns rolling the dice and choosing one of the two numbers to turn up on the dice for the down row and the other number for the top row (i.e., if they roll a 2 and a 4, they can go 2 down and 4 across or they can choose to go 4 down and 2 across). They will select the card that corresponds with their roll, read the question, and answer it. After a card has been used, set it aside and fill the spot with a new card. You may wish to use the cards from the "2" deck to add deeper questions to the mix at some point.

Discussion Prompts

1. Did you enjoy having the opportunity to share about yourself?
2. Did you prefer the questions from the "1" pile or the "2" pile? Why?
3. What did you learn about someone in the group that you didn't already know?

Variations

➲ Lay the cards face up. Allow them to read the questions before choosing which number they will use for the down row and which number for across.

Odd or Even Match Up

Objective
To create a non-threatening environment for individuals to answer questions and share more openly about themselves.

Who
Individuals who share more openly through the portal of a game than they would if simply asked a question.

Group Size
1 or more (8 or less is ideal)

Materials
➲ The UNGAME cards

Description
Using either the "1" pile or the deeper questions in the "2" pile, lay down the cards in rows five across and five deep on the table face down. Group members take turns flipping two cards over and looking at the small numbers in the lower right-hand corner of each card. If the two numbers are both even (or both odd), they can choose which question they would like to answer. If two cards are turned over and the numbers are odd and even, the group gets to decide which of the two questions they would like for the person to answer. After a card has been used and the question has been answered replace that spot with a new card from the pile of extra cards.

Discussion Prompts
1. What types of questions are you most comfortable answering about yourself?
2. Do you enjoy having the opportunity to share about yourself? Why or why not?
3. What did you learn about someone in the group that you didn't already know?

Challenge Your Opponent

Objective
To create a non-threatening environment where individuals can answer questions and share more openly about themselves.

Who
Individuals who share more openly through the portal of a game than they would if simply asked a question.

Group Size
3 to 12 is ideal

Materials
➲ The UNGAME cards

Description
Hand out five cards to each person from either the "1" or the "2" pile, and put the remaining cards in a draw pile in the middle of the group. Group members take turns choosing one of the questions they have in their hand to ask to the entire group. Any group member who chooses to answer the question can earn a point for themselves. The person with most points in the end gets a chance to be on the "hot seat" where other group members take turns giving compliments to this person. It is possible that every member of the group will answer every question and have the same number of points so everyone will earn the chance to be on the "hot seat".

Discussion Prompts
1. Why did you choose to answer as many questions as you did?
2. Did you want the chance to be in the "hot seat", or not? Why?
3. How do you feel when others are giving you compliments?
4. How do you feel when you give others compliments?
5. What did you learn about someone else?
6. What did you discover about yourself?

Pick a Number!

Objective
To create a non-threatening environment where individuals can answer questions and share more openly about themselves.

Who
Individuals who share more openly through the portal of a game than they would if simply asked a question.

Group Size
2 or more

Materials
➲ The UNGAME cards

Description
Select either the "1" or the "2" cards. Divide the group into two equal teams. Each team selects one person for each round to go against a member of the other team. The leader selects a card and looks at the number on the lower right-hand corner. It will be a number between 1 and 70. The representative from each team selects a number between 1 and 70. Then the person who guesses closest to the number on the card is given the chance to answer the question to earn two points for his or her team. The other person can answer the same question for a chance to earn one point for his or her team. Play several rounds of this game, giving everyone a chance to be the team representative.

Discussion Prompts
1. Was this game fair? Why or why not?
2. How much of your life is based on random chances, like this game is?
3. Do you wish you could have been the person answering every question?
4. Do you like to have the spotlight on you? Why or why not?
5. What did you learn about a member of the group that you didn't already know?

Variation
➲ Award a bonus point to anyone who guesses the exact number on the card.

Journey

Objective
To create a non-threatening environment where individuals can answer questions and share more openly about themselves.

Who
Individuals who share more openly through the portal of a game than they would if simply asked a question.

Group Size
2 or more

Materials
- The UNGAME cards
- 1 Die
- 1 small item that can be used as a marker (beads, crayons, coins, playing pieces from another game, etc.)

Description
Make a path using the UNGAME cards by laying them out end to end in a circle pattern with the cards facing down (lay out more cards if you wish to play for a longer period of time, less for less time). You may use the "1" or the "2" cards or both for this activity. Give each player a playing piece (this can be anything from a small bead to a coin to a crayon, etc.). Designate one card as the start. Each player takes a turn rolling the die and moving that many spaces. When a player lands on a card that's facing down, he or she then turns it over and reads the question and can choose to answer it or not. If they choose to not answer it, then it is turned face down. If they choose to answer it, then it remains face up. Each player takes a turn rolling the die and landing on a card. If the card is already face up, then the player can answer it if they wish but there's no reward for doing so. The goal of the game is for the group to get all of the cards turned over before the designated time limit is up.

Discussion Prompts

1. Did you enjoy having the opportunity to share about yourself?
2. If a card was face up, why did you choose to answer or to not answer the question?
3. What did you learn about someone in the group that you didn't already know?

Variations

➲ Create two circles and have two teams playing at the same time. Each group tries to turn all of the cards in their circle over before the other team does.

Stacks

Objective
To create a non-threatening environment where individuals can answer questions and share more openly about themselves.

Who
Individuals who share more openly through the portal of a game than they would if simply asked a question.

Group Size
1 or more

Materials
➲ The UNGAME cards
➲ 1 Die
➲ 1 playing piece (This can be anything that is used as a marker)

Description
    Count out six stacks of five cards each and place them on the table. Roll the die and move a playing piece on top of the stacks starting with Stack 1, then moving down the line to Stack 6, and then back to the first one. When the player lands on a stack, he or she turns over the top card and reads the question. The individual who reads the question can then choose to eliminate that card by answering the question, or they can choose not to answer it and place the card in a reject pile. If they reject the card, they must replace it with a new card from the extra cards. If the group can eliminate one complete stack of cards before a set time limit, offer a prize (extra free time, stickers, candy, etc.).

Discussion Prompts

1. Did you prefer for it to be your turn or someone else's turn when playing this game? Why?
2. Are you comfortable answering questions about yourself? Why or why not?
3. What did you learn about someone you didn't already know?

Variation

➲ Once a stack is eliminated, then move the game piece on top of the remaining piles. Once the group is down to one stack, they don't have to roll the die anymore. If they eliminate all of the cards in all six stacks, offer a bonus prize.

One or Two?

Objective
To compare the difference between lighthearted and deeper questions, and to explore feelings people have about answering different types of questions.

Who
People that often give surfaced answers who could benefit from being more open when asked deeper questions.

Group Size
1 or more

Materials
➲ The UNGAME cards

Description
Mix the "1" and "2" cards together into one pile with the question side up. Gather the group into a circle. The leader takes a card from the top of the pile, and without showing the group if it has a "1" or a "2" on the other side, he or she reads the question. The group has to decide if they think it's a more lighthearted question and has a "1" on it, or if it's a deeper "2" question. After they decide what number card they think it is, the leader reveals the number. Then the leader asks the group the question (this question can be for anyone to answer or for a specific individual the leader chooses). If the group was able to identify the type of question it was, then they receive a point. If they don't choose correctly, then the leader earns the point. If in the end the leader has more points, then the group has to sing a silly song (or do something silly the leader states). If the group earns more points, they get to choose a silly song for the leader to sing (or something similar).

Discussion Prompts

1. How could you tell if a question was lighthearted or deeper?
2. Which type of questions do you like to answer more?
3. How often do you ask people lighthearted questions?
4. How often do you ask people deeper questions?
5. How often do you give surfaced answers to questions?
6. Why do we sometimes give surfaced answers to deep questions?

Guess the Answer!

Objective
To create a non-threatening environment where individuals can answer questions and share more openly about themselves.

Who
Individuals who share more openly through the portal of a game than they would if simply asked a question.

Group Size
1 or more

Materials
- The UNGAME cards
- Paper
- Pens or pencils

Description
Select one person who chooses a question card and reads it out loud to the group. The person who reads the question then writes down his or her answer to the question, in one sentence, on a piece of paper. The remaining group members write down one sentence trying to guess the answer the person who read the question has written down. After everyone is finished writing down their answer, the person who read the question reveals their answer. Group members compare the answer they wrote to what the person said. This game can played just for fun or award points to those who guessed closest to the answer for an added fun competition.

Discussion Prompts
1. Were you surprised by the answers others thought you would give?
2. Do you feel that the members of the group know you very well?
3. If you feel that group members don't know you very well, is this something you would like to change?

One or the Other

Objective
To create a non-threatening environment where individuals can answer questions and share more openly about themselves.

Who
Individuals who share more openly through the portal of a game than they would if simply asked a question.

Group Size
2 or more

Materials
➲   The UNGAME cards

Description
Lay out two questions face up, one that is a "1" card and one that is a "2" card. Ask individuals to choose which question they would rather answer (without letting them know which one is which). After answering the question, reveal if they earned 1 point or 2 based the card they chose.

Discussion Prompts
1. Why did you choose your question?
2. Do you prefer to answer lighthearted questions or deeper questions? Why?
3. How can it benefit you if you're willing to share in a deeper way with others?

MONOPOLY

The MONOPOLY game is one of the most popular games ever made. The games found in this chapter are designed to fit into a shorter time frame than it would take normally to complete a full game. Sometimes just the pieces or money are used for an activity and other times the entire game is used.

Game Summary

Everyone starts the MONOPOLY game with the same amount of money. Through the process of landing on property spaces, and buying those property cards, players have a chance to earn money as others land on the property they own. Once a set of properties is owned, the individual who owns them can buy houses and hotels to add to the property to make it worth more, and the people who land on the property have to pay more. The winner is the wealthiest player in the end.

Therapeutic Application of MONOPOLY

Playing the MONOPOLY game requires patience, luck, and also some strategy. In the end, it may seem that the one taking everyone else's property can become like a power-hungry person filled with greed who delights in seeing others fall. Lessons can be pulled about feelings related to taking from others or having to give up what you have.

Discussion Prompts: Greed

1. How did you feel during this game when you were able to take money or property away from others?
2. How did you feel if you had to give up all of your property and money in the end?
3. In your life experience, have you ever met people who seem to be full of greed? What does this look like?
4. Is it OK to want more for yourself?

5. When does wanting more for yourself turn from a good thing to a bad thing?
6. Have you ever noticed greed taking control of your own life?
7. How can we deal with feelings of greed when they enter your life?

Discussion Prompts: Giving up what you have when you can't afford it

1. In your life experience, have you ever had to hand over the property you have to others or stop engaging in certain activities because you could no longer afford it? How did this make you feel?
2. If you have experienced giving up things, how did you deal with it?
3. Do you blame others and become angry when in this situation? Is this healthy for you?
4. What can you do to improve your own situation when you find yourself having to give up things you can no longer afford?

MONOPOLY
Games

Money for Me

Objective
For individuals to recognize the benefits of filling their free time with healthy activities as opposed to negative ones.

Who
People who make poor choices with how they spend their free time.

Group Size
2 to 8 is ideal (but the game could be used with a larger group if done in teams – see variation)

Materials
➲ The MONOPOLY game
➲ A copy of the *List of Activities* (found on the following page)

Description
Lay out the game board but don't give anyone any of the money. Each person takes turns rolling and moving around the board, but for this game there is no buying of property. Instead, individuals collect the amount of money listed on each property as they move around the board. Each person should go around the board once and try to collect as much money as possible. When landing on a spot that isn't a property, there is no money collected. When they make it all the way around, they can collect $200 when they get to "go."

After everyone has a pile of money, hand out the sheet of what they can use their money to "purchase." Allow time for everyone to decide what activities they would choose. Then discuss the need to fill your spare time with healthy activities and using them as a coping device instead of filling free time with negative behavior.

Discussion Prompts

1. Why did you choose to buy the activities you chose?
2. What activities were not on the list that you wish were?
3. How do you usually spend your free time?
4. Why is it important to be able to find positive activities you can do during your free time?
5. What would you do with your free time if money was unlimited?
6. What can you do in your free time with the budget you have in your own life?
7. How can changing what you do in your free time help you cope with difficult situations?

Variation

➲ Play the game in teams. Each group must decide what they would buy with their money. The group may split the money so each person gets a certain amount, or you may ask them to work together to decide what it is they want as a group.

➲ Add negative options to the list (cigarettes, drugs, alcohol, etc.) to help group members make healthy choices even when negative choices are an option.

List of Activities

Free
Trip to library
Walking or running
Volunteer at your favorite charity
Go to church
Watch TV
Time on Internet

$20
Frisbee
Books
Magazines
Stationery and pens
Journal and pens
Coffee date with a friend
LEGO products
Ice cream with a friend

$50
Movie tickets
Art supplies
Music on CDs or downloads
Cooking ingredients and supplies
Lunch date with a friend
Tennis racquet and balls
Gas money for your car

$100
Yoga classes
New video games
Donate to charity
Camping trip

$200
Sign up for a sports team
A new cell phone

$300
Dog
Musical instrument
New Video game console
New MP3 music system

$400
Membership to a gym

$500
Vacation to a city
Vacation to a beach

Rich vs. Poor

Objective
To understand how we react to the situations we are born into and to recognize ways to improve our own situation.

Who
Individuals who think they're victims of their own circumstances and who could benefit from looking at ways to improve their situation.

Group Size
4 to 8 is ideal (but could have more if have bigger teams)

Materials
➲ The MONOPOLY game

Description
Place one card from each of the property groups in a pile. Shuffle the pile and evenly distribute the cards to the group members. If there are extra properties, have group members roll the die and the highest roller gets to select an extra property. Continue until one card from each property group has been distributed. Once everyone has their cards, give them the other properties that go with their set(s). Each card set in the game should belong to someone.

Money is distributed based on the amount of money each property would cost to buy (e.g., the person with Boardwalk and Park Place would start the game with $750 – the amounts listed on the board).

The railroads and utilities are up for grabs if anyone wants to buy them when landing on those spaces. The game can be played using the Chance and Community Chest Cards or simply make those free spaces.

Now, play a regular game with each person moving around the board. At the end of the game, discuss the feelings individuals have towards those who started with less and those who started the game with more.

Discussion Prompts

1. Did you feel that one player had an advantage over the others in this game? If so, how did this make you feel?
2. Do you ever look at what others have and get jealous? If so, why do you think you have these feelings?
3. What do you usually do if you find yourself in a situation where you feel that you're at a disadvantage compared to others?
4. Is there a way to move yourself into a situation where you have more security in your life than you have now? What will it take for you to do this?
5. What changes can you make in your life to change your current situation?

Variation

➲ Focus the questions on anger management issues if you have individuals who react with anger when others have more than them.

Job Hunt

Objective
For people to think about their future and to set goals as to what career they would like to pursue.

Who
People who have little ambition for their future career who could benefit from exploring career options.

Group Size
4 to 8 is ideal

Materials
- ➲ The MONOPOLY game
- ➲ Sticky Notes (The regular size ones cut in half down the middle are perfect.)
- ➲ Pens or pencils

Description
Using 18 sheets of Sticky Notes, cut them in half down the middle so there are 36 total. Evenly distribute the notes to each player. Ask the players to write down one job on each note that they think would be interesting to learn more about, or that they would like to have one day.

Play the game of MONOPOLY but don't hand out any money at the beginning. When a player lands on a property space, they can choose which job they would like to place on that space and stick it to the board. They should also look at the amount of money that is listed on the space (the amount to buy the property) and write it on the note. This is the amount of money they earn for that job during the game. Anyone who lands on this space earns that amount of money (including the first person to put the note down). Any space without a money amount (Chance or Community Chest) earns $100. Corner spaces are free spaces.

At some point, a player who has used up all their job notes may land on a space which has no job on it. They can ask to "borrow" someone else's note that hasn't been used yet and place it on the space.

Play until all the spaces are filled or you run out of money in the bank. The person with the most money at the end is declared the "winner."

Discussion Prompts

1. Of all the jobs that people came up with, which one appeals to you the most?
2. Which job do you think you'll most likely have someday?
3. What should you be doing now to insure that you'll be able to have the career that you want for yourself someday?

Variations

➲ Have group members say how they feel about working at that job as they land on the spot.

➲ The leader creates a board filled with jobs ahead of time by using Sticky Notes to cover the existing properties. The game is then played using the rules set up above.

➲ If anyone lands on the jail space, they have to pay $200 to cover the lawyer's fee to get out. If there is a "lawyer" note on the board, they must pay $200 to the player who is closest to that space at the time.

Game Piece Challenge

Objective
For people to brainstorm ways to spend free time engaged in healthy activities, rather than the destructive activities they may currently be involved in.

Who
People who need to change the way they use their free time.

Group Size
1 or more

Materials
- The MONOPOLY game
- Paper and pens
- Envelopes
- A copy of the *Game Piece Activity List*

Description
   Place each playing piece from the MONOPOLY game into an envelope with a strip of paper. The paper should have a description of what type of activities the piece represents. Give each person a sheet of paper and pen, and talk about how engaging in healthy activities can be helpful for dealing with life difficulties or a way to fill free time with things other than destructive behaviors.

   Pass the envelopes around. Give a set time limit (30 seconds works well) for individuals to write down as many activities as they can think of that fit the category for the piece in their envelope. Pass the pieces around the group at the time interval. This can be done in teams if you have a larger group.

   After everyone has completed their list, ask individuals to share what they wrote. They will earn one point for each activity they have on their list that nobody else listed. Discuss the lists that the group came up with and the need to find healthy activities.

Discussion Prompts

1. Why were some of the categories easier to think of activities for than others?
2. Were there any activities listed that you haven't ever done but would like to do?
3. What stops you from doing some of the things you want to do?
4. How would it benefit you to engage in new activities with new groups of people?

Game Piece Activity List

Shoe: Activities that involve walking or running.

Spinning wheel: Activities that promote education and getting a good job.

Money bag: Activities you can do if you have extra money.

Wheelbarrow: Activities to do in the yard.

Car: Activities that involve travel.

Iron: Activities that promote improvement (home cleaning, organizing, remodeling).

Horse: Outdoor farm or wilderness and mountain type of activities.

Thimble: Arts and crafts type activities.

Dog: Activities you can do with a pet.

Boat: Activities you can do in or around the water.

Money for Moving

Objective
For people to determine if engaging in a fitness activity has an effect on how they feel physically and/or emotionally. To encourage people to engage in exercise to improve their own mental and physical strength.

Who
People who could benefit from exercise.

Group Size
2 or more

Materials
- ➲ MONOPOLY game money
- ➲ Small prizes that can be bought with the money (stickers, pencils, snacks, etc.). Or you can offer extra free time, movie time, etc., that they can earn.

Description
Show the group the prizes that they have the opportunity to purchase, and put a price on each prize (based on how many prizes you have and how many people you have in your group). Offer group members the opportunity to earn MONOPOLY game money to buy these prizes by engaging in various exercises. Announce the first exercise (e.g., everyone who does 20 jumping jacks will earn $20). After giving them the chance to engage in the exercise, give out money to anyone who completed the task. Continue in this manner until you feel you have passed out enough money for group members to buy the prizes you've offered.

Discussion Prompts

1. How can exercising regularly benefit you emotionally?
2. How can improving your fitness level benefit you?
3. What are some ways you like to work out?
4. How often do you work out?
5. What can you do to add more exercise to your daily routine?

Variations

- Instead of doing exercise to earn money, offer them the chance to answer questions about themselves, give compliments to others, or say things that they like about themselves to earn money.
- Instead of giving out prizes, play this as a team competition, and the team that accumulates the most money wins the game.
- Use the list from the game *Physical Puzzle* (found on page 226) to find exercise options for this game.

Money Dash

Objective

For people to discuss how they deal with feelings about having to work harder for money than others do who earn the same amount of money.

Who

People who are focused on how life is "unfair," and have feelings of resentment and anger because of this.

Group Size

2 or more

Materials

➲ MONOPOLY game money

Description

This is a relay race to collect the correct amount of money before the other team does. Set up the room so that there is a desk or table at one end that has a pile of Monopoly® money on it (but only include one of the $500 bills). There should be room to walk from one end of the room to the desk. Divide the group into two teams. Have each team line up in single file lines at the opposite end of the room from where the desk with the money is.

The leader will give a dollar amount that each team must collect that is more than $500 but less than $1,000 (e.g., $784 or $946). Each team sends one person at a time who walks/runs to the table and collects one piece of money at a time (the first person to take the $500 bill will have gained a big advantage for his or her team). After the first person in each line brings back a piece of money, the next person from each team can go and collect a piece of money for his or her team. Some people may have to go through the line twice in order to collect enough money for their team to add up to the given dollar amount.

If a team collects too much money, at the end they must send one piece of money back at a time and leave it there. Then the next person in line may collect a new piece of money. The first team to gather the correct amount of money wins the round. Put the money back into the pile at the end of each round and give a new dollar amount for the next round.

Discussion Prompts
1. What happened when one team collected the $500 bill first?
2. How did you feel if you were on the team that had to work harder to collect the first $500 by gathering smaller bills – one at a time?
3. Do you ever feel that your life is unfair because it seems like you have to work harder for your money than others do?
4. If you feel that it is unfair, how do you deal with these feelings?
5. Does having more money than others make you feel important?
6. Do you feel left behind when you're with people who have more money than you have?
7. What do you spend your extra money on? Why?
8. Can you be happy if you have less money than others?
9. Can you be unhappy if you have more money than others?
10. How can you find balance in your life when it comes to earning money?

Variation
➲ For each round, the winning team gets to keep their money. At the end of the game, hold a small auction of prizes or snacks that the two teams can bid for against each other.

APPLES TO APPLES

APPLES TO APPLES is one of the best group games out there. One of the biggest advantages of this game is that people can join in during the middle of the game. This makes it a great option to have ongoing during a free time for any group. It's very easy to show newcomers how to play, and the game will quickly become a favorite for those who try it.

Game Summary

APPLES TO APPLES comes with 756 Red Apple Cards and 252 Green Apple Cards. The Red Apple Cards are mostly filled with people, places, things, and events. The Green Apple Cards contain descriptive words.

Everyone begins with seven red cards, and one person is chosen to be the "judge" for the first round. The judge selects a green card from the top of the draw pile, and he or she lays it out on the table face up so everyone can see the word. Each person (except for the judge) looks at their seven cards. The players then select the one card in their hand that they think best fits the descriptive word and lays it face down in a pile in the middle. Once everyone has laid down a card, the judge collects the pile and reads them. The judge determines which one he or she thinks best fits the descriptive word and announces this card to the group. The person who played that card is the winner of the round and collects the green card.

For the next round, select a new judge (usually you will go around the circle). Everyone takes a red card from the draw pile to start each round with seven cards. The judge lays down another green card and play continues in the same manner as above. The winner is the first one to collect a predetermined number of green cards or the person who has the most green cards when it is time to end the game.

Therapeutic Applications of APPLES TO APPLES

APPLES TO APPLES is such an interactive game that many different object lessons can be pulled from playing the game itself.

Oftentimes people will feel that the judge didn't make the choice that made the most sense; they'll frequently think that their card should have been chosen when it wasn't. This can lead to a discussion about feeling like life is fair or not. Because the judge is the one in control, there's a good opportunity to discuss feelings we have about being in control or feeling like others are in control. Also, everyone should feel the pressure of being the judge, and this can open the discussion about making decisions when in a group. Being judged by others or our own judgment of others is another easy lesson that can be derived from this game.

Many of the games in this chapter focus on self-discovery. Individuals are asked to select cards in the course of the game that are descriptive of how they see themselves, how they think others view them, or how group members view each other. Some of the games focus more on communication skills or self-esteem. As you'll see, there is such a wide variety of ways that APPLES TO APPLES can be used as a therapeutic tool to open up communication in a group.

Discussion Prompts: Feeling like life isn't fair

1. Did you ever feel it wasn't fair when your card was not chosen and it clearly seemed to be the best fit? Why?
2. How do you react when you feel that your life isn't fair?
3. Do you feel that other people have an advantage over you in life? If so, why do you feel you're at a disadvantage?
4. If you feel that your life is unfair, who do you blame?
5. Do you feel that you can rise above the circumstances that seem to be putting you at an unfair advantage?
6. What can you do to overcome circumstances you feel put you in an unfair situation?

Discussion Prompts: Feeling like others control your life

1. How did you feel when someone else was deciding if you had a good card or not?
2. Do you ever feel like others judge the decisions you make? How does this make you feel?

3. Do you question your own judgment when someone else doesn't think you made the right choice about something?
4. How can you become more confident with yourself when your decision isn't what others agree with?

Discussion Prompts: Making decisions

1. Do you prefer to be the one leading and making decisions, or following? Why?
2. Do you ever feel that the options in front of you are all negative? How can you turn your negatives into positives?
3. Did you ever argue to convince the judge that your card was best? Why or why not? Are you willing to stand up and fight for what you believe?
4. Did you ever feel the judge made a decision that you felt wasn't fair? Why or why not? How do you feel inside when you think things are unfair?

Discussion Prompts: Judging others or feeling judged

1. Do you ever feel that people judge you? Is this a good or bad thing, and why?
2. What information do you use to judge others? Why do we judge others?
3. Did you ever select a card from the draw pile that would have been perfect for a previous round?
4. Did you wish you could go back and get a "do over" on the previous round with a new card?
5. Do you ever wish you could get a "do over" in life?
6. What would you go back and change in your life?
7. What can you do about situations you wish you could do over but can't?
8. Would you want the job of permanent judge for this game? Why or why not?
9. Would you want to play with one person having all the power? Why or why not?

THERAPY GAMES

APPLES TO APPLES Games

Apple Answers

Objective
For people to express how they're feeling in a non-threatening manner. For people to get to know others in the group.

Who
People who have trouble sharing and expressing their feelings and emotions.

Group Size
2 or more

Materials
➲ APPLES TO APPLES game
➲ A copy or copies of the question list (Make your own or use the *Find a card...* provided with this game.)
➲ Optional: Poster board

Description
Prior to this activity, create a list of six to eight questions that group members must answer (see the *Find a card...* list for ideas). You may want to post the questions on a poster board or provide each person with a copy of the questions for themselves.

Spread out the red and green cards on the table. Allow time for each person in the group to select individual cards to go with each question on the list. Once everyone has collected all of their cards, allow time for each member to share their answers with the group.

Discussion Prompts
1. What did you learn about someone else that you didn't already know?
2. Were some of the questions more difficult to find cards for? Why?
3. Do you think someone who knows you well would have selected the same cards to describe you as you did? Why?

4. Do you tend to describe your life in a positive manner or negative? Why?
5. How could your life change if you simply viewed it in a more positive manner?

Find a card...
Something you love
Something you hate
How would your friends describe you?
How would your family describe you?
How would you like people to describe you?
That describes how your week has gone?
Of a place you would like to go to for a vacation
Who is someone you'd like to have lunch with? (A time machine is available.)
How do you see your future?
How would you describe the way you deal with anger?

Who Is It?

Objective
To learn how others in the group see themselves and to share how you view yourself.

Who
People who have difficulty sharing about themselves but could do so more easily through an activity. Groups who are familiar with each other.

Group Size
4 to 12 is ideal

Materials
- APPLES TO APPLES game
- Paper
- Pens or pencils
- A copy of the question list

Description
Lay out the game cards (green and red) on the table. Ask each person to select three cards that answer the questions on a list (the leader should come up these questions prior to the activity). For example, the questions may be:

1. Which card describes who you are?
2. Which card has the name of a person who would fit in with your family?
3. Which card is about something you think would be fun?

The players should keep their cards secret and in the same order as the questions posted. Each player sets their cards on the table as a separate pile. The leader then gathers up the piles of cards and lays them out on the table so the answers are revealed. (In doing so, the leader needs to keep the cards in the same order so they match the questions. Also, each pile should remain separate.) Each person tries to guess whose pile each one is, and they write down their answers.

After everyone records their answers, find out which pile belonged to which person. Give one point for each one that was guessed correctly. Allow time for people to explain why they selected the cards they did. Also, have people talk about why they thought the pile belonged to the person they guessed.

Discussion Prompts
1. What did you learn about someone in the group that you didn't know before?
2. Would it have been easier or more difficult to answer the questions without the cards? Why?
3. Why is it important to have people in your life who know who you really are on the inside?
4. Do you have very many people in your life who you feel really know you?
5. Do you have a desire for others to get to know you more than they do? Why or why not?
6. How can you open up more so others get to know you?

Variations
➲ Only have one question for the people to answer rather than three.
➲ Play by the rules listed in this game but instead of the leader reading all of the cards, gather up the piles and hand one pile out to each person. The group members take turns reading the cards to the group.

Truth or Lie?

Objective
To share how you view yourself in a non-threatening manner.

Who
People who have a hard time sharing openly about how they view themselves. Groups who could benefit from getting to know one another at a deeper level

Group Size
4 to 15 is ideal

Materials
➲ APPLES TO APPLES game

Description
Spread the red and green cards out on the table. Each person selects three cards that they would use to describe themselves (the truth); they also pick out three cards that are the opposite of who they are (a lie). (Both the truth and the lie can be green or red cards.) Each person should have their own two sets of cards in two piles face down in front of them. Nobody else in the group knows which pile is a truth and which one is a lie.

Starting with one member of the group, the leader randomly selects one of the piles (or the person sitting next to them can do this as well) and asks the person to turn those cards over for all to see. The group members then vote "truth" or "lie" based on which pile they think was revealed. Voting can be done by asking or by using the green and red cards to vote (any green or red card will do). Simply place a red card down on the table if it is thought to be a lie and green if it seems to be true. Give one point to anyone who guesses correctly. After each turn, ask to see the opposite pile and have the person explain why they selected the cards they did.

Discussion Prompts
1. Why did you select the cards you did?
2. Was it harder to find cards that were true about yourself or ones that were lies? Why?
3. Was it hard for you to find positive things about yourself?
4. Do you feel that you're bragging if you are asked to state positive things about yourself?
5. What did you learn about another member of the group that you didn't already know? Were you surprised to learn this information?

Variation
➲ Instead of asking for "truth and lie" cards, tell the group members to find three cards of things they like and three cards of things they don't like.

Majority Wins

Objective
To learn how others view us as individuals.

Who
Groups who are familiar with each other. Individuals who could benefit from learning how others view them.

Group Size
4 to 12 is ideal

Materials
- ➲ APPLES TO APPLES game (You may wish to select only positive green cards to use for this activity.)
- ➲ 3x5 index cards
- ➲ Pens

Description
Everyone in the group needs to have a set of 3x5 index cards with each group member's name on a separate card. Using the green descriptive cards, lay one out at a time. The group members select the name of the person they think best fits the descriptive word. They then lay this index card face down so others cannot see their answer. Everyone reveals their answer at the same time. One point is awarded to each individual who guesses with the majority (those who choose the person who is selected by the most members of the group). Points may be recorded by handing out red game cards.

Discussion Prompts
1. Were you surprised when others in the group selected your name for any of the descriptive words? If so, which words and why?
2. How do you feel about the words others selected to describe you?
3. Is it easy for you to hear positive feedback from others?

4. How would this game have been different if negative descriptive cards were laid out?
5. How easy was it for you to select which group member matched with each word?
6. Do you feel that you are able to figure other people out easily? How can this observation skill help you?

This Is Me

Objective
To learn how others view us as individuals. To create an opportunity to discuss how we see ourselves versus how others see us.

Who
Individuals who could benefit from learning how others view them. Group members who are familiar with each other.

Group Size
4 to 12 is ideal

Materials
- ⊃ APPLES TO APPLES game
- ⊃ 3x5 index cards
- ⊃ Markers

Description
Each person should write his or her own name on a blank 3x5 index card. They then put these cards all into one pile. Using only the green cards from the game, deal out ten cards to each person. Select one name from the pile of name cards and place it face up on the table. This person becomes the judge for this round. Everyone else must select the best card in their own hand that would describe that person on the card and places it face down on the table. The judge then collects the cards and picks the descriptive green card that they feel best describes himself or herself. The person who put that card down on the table earns one point and can collect the name card from the table. The person who collects the most name cards at the end is declared the winner.

Discussion Prompts

1. Was it easy or difficult for you to select a card from the pile that described yourself?
2. Is it hard for you to accept what others say about you?
3. Do you most often hear positive or negative comments to describe you from others?
4. Do you give yourself positive or negative comments most often? Why?
5. What is the advantage of hearing positive comments from others or from yourself?
6. How often do you give positive comments to others?

Variations

➲ Go through the green cards prior to this activity and pull out the negative cards so only positive cards are selected.
➲ After everyone gets their ten cards, allow them to trade a certain number of cards with the pile before each round.

Apples Debate

Objective
To clearly communicate your ideas and feelings about why your answer is the right one. To learn to stand up for your own ideas by using clear communication skills.

Who
People who could benefit from learning to stand up for themselves. Also, people who need to learn to communicate their own side of the story in a clear and positive manner.

Group Size
4 or more

Materials
➲ APPLES TO APPLES game
➲ 3x5 index cards

Description
Follow the directions to the APPLES TO APPLES game. However, instead of laying the red cards on the table, each player holds on to their own card. When it is time to reveal their choice, they must present their case as to why their card should win. The judge must select the person who presents the best argument, instead of determining which card they think matches the green card the best.

Discussion Prompts
1. Do you feel confident when standing up for what you believe in? Why or why not?
2. When is it beneficial to be able to stand up for what you believe in and state your case clearly?
3. How do you feel when it seems that others hold a belief that is different than yours?

4. Do you ever feel tension when you argue your case with others? What does this do to your ability to state your case clearly?
5. Are you able to listen clearly to what others say when they have a different opinion than you do? Or do you think more about what you want to say next?
6. What is a positive way to argue your point? What is a negative way?

Variations

➲ Set a time limit for how long each person can state their case.
➲ The entire group becomes a jury. Everyone must vote for the person who presents the best argument on why his or her card should be selected. Each group member gets one vote in this process and cannot vote for his or her own card. Give everyone a 3x5 index card with the name of each group member on it that they can use to vote with.

Story Challenge

Objective
To practice clear communication skills. To practice listening and reasoning skills.

Who
Individuals who need to work on communicating clearly. Individuals who need to work on improving their listening skills.

Group Size
4 to 12 is ideal

Materials
- APPLES TO APPLES game
- 3x5 index cards
- Markers

Description
Hand out three of the red game cards to each person in the group. Participants take turns telling a fictional story that contains the words on the three cards that were handed out to them. When a card is used in a story, it should be shown to the group and placed on the table. The story can't be longer than one minute. After every group member has shared their story, the participants vote for the one that was the best.

Discussion Prompts
1. Was it easy for you to think of a story quickly?
2. Is it easy for you to think of what to say when in a conversation with others?
3. Was it easy to listen to the other stories before it was your turn? Or did you think about what you were going to say when it was your turn?

4. How often do you really listen to others instead of thinking of what you're going to say next?
5. How can you tell if someone is really listening to you?
6. How can you show others that you are listening?
7. How can it benefit you to improve your ability to listen to others?

Continuing Story

Objective
To practice using clear speaking skills and proper listening skills.

Who
Individuals who need to practice speaking clearly in front of groups. Individuals who need to practice listening to others without interrupting them and also to be able to show a clear understanding of what others say.

Group Size
4 to 12 is ideal

Materials
⮑ APPLES TO APPLES game

Description
Give everyone in the group one random game card and have the group sit in a circle. One person starts a fictional story that contains the word on the given card, and he or she can only share for 30 seconds. Go around the circle in this manner, with each person adding more to the story while using the word on his or her card.

Discussion Prompts
1. Why was it important to use clear listening skills when playing this game?
2. Do you get easy distracted when listening to others?
3. What do you miss out on when you don't focus on what others are saying?
4. What can you do to improve your listening skills?
5. Was it easy or difficult for you to formulate your story?
6. Why was it important to be able to speak clearly to others when you want to get your ideas across to them?
7. What can you do to improve your communication skills?

Variations

➲ Make the time limit for sharing longer than 30 seconds.

➲ Give each person more than one card. Everyone must use all their cards when it is their turn (or go around the circle more than once and each time a new card should be used).

What's the Word?

Objective
To encourage interactive conversation among group members. To encourage the use of proper communication skills.

Who
People who need to practice engaging in appropriate, interactive conversation with others. People who need to be encouraged to open up to others through communication.

Group Size
3 or more

Materials
➲ APPLES TO APPLES game

Description
Select one person to be "it." Ask this person to turn his or her back to the group. The remaining group members select one game card for the entire group. Each person in the group looks at the card to see what the word or phrase is; however, do not reveal this to the person who is "it." The person chosen to be "it" turns around. He or she then engages in a discussion with the group, during which the other members try to get him or her to say the "secret" word or phrase. The group may ask the person questions, engage the person in conversation, or whatever else they can think of to prompt the saying of what is on the card. The individual who doesn't know tries to talk as much as possible without saying the word or phrase from the card. Do several rounds of this game, giving different people a chance to be "it."

Discussion Prompts

1. Do you enjoy talking with other people?
2. Who do you like to talk with the most and why?
3. Do you wish you had more people in your life that you could talk with?
4. Do you wish you could talk about things in your life more easily?
5. Do people ever try to get you to tell them your secrets? Who? Why?
6. Would it help you to tell your secrets to others?
7. With which individuals do you share your secrets and why?
8. Why don't you share your secrets with others?

Apple Awards

Objective
For group members to recognize the positive traits that exist in each other.

Who
People who could benefit from hearing positive comments about themselves. Group members should be familiar with each other.

Group Size
2 or more

Materials
➲ APPLES TO APPLES game

Description
Have the group sit in a circle and spread the game cards out in the middle. Ask each person to think about the person who is sitting to their right. Then have everyone select a card that represents an award they would like to give to that person. The word on the card should be symbolic of what they see in this individual. For example, a card that reads "The Olympics" can be given to someone "because you're good at sports," or a card that reads "Brains" to someone "because you're so smart."

Discussion Prompts
1. How do you feel about the word that was chosen to describe you?
2. Were you surprised by the award you were given? Why or why not?
3. Is it easy or hard to think of positive things about others? Why?
4. Is it easy or hard to think of positive things about yourself? Why?

Variation
➲ Have group members select an award for themselves as well.

Aspire

Objective
To look ahead to the future and set positive goals.

Who
Members of a group who could benefit from getting to know each other at a deeper level. Individuals who would benefit from making future goals for themselves.

Group Size
4 to 12 is ideal

Materials
➲ APPLES TO APPLES game

Description
Spread out some of the red and green cards on a table. Ask the group members to find one to three cards that describe what they aspire to be in five, ten, and/or twenty years. Have each person explain their choices to the group after everyone has selected their cards.

Discussion Prompts
1. Do you think about your future and where you want to be in life?
2. Why is it beneficial to picture a positive future for yourself?
3. What can you do to make sure your goals and dreams come true?

Opposite

Objective
To prompt discussion on how individuals view themselves.

Who
Individuals who have difficulty sharing about how they view themselves. Groups of individuals who could benefit from getting to know each other at a deeper level.

Group Size
3 to 10 is ideal

Materials
➲ APPLES TO APPLES game

Description
Spread the red and green cards out on a table. Ask everyone to select three different cards; two should be truthful about how they view themselves and one should be the opposite of that. Each person should lay his or her cards out on the table so all the others in the group can see. Take turns guessing which card is the one that is opposite. Award points to anyone who correctly guesses the "opposite" card.

Discussion Prompts
1. Was it easy for you to determine the opposite card and the true one for each individual?
2. Was it easy for others to figure out what was the opposite of who you really are?
3. Do you think others know the true you? Why or why not?
4. Do you have a desire for others to know the real you more than they do? Why or why not?
5. Would it be a benefit for others to get to know you more?
6. How can you share more about yourself in a positive way so that others can get to know you?

LET'S GO FISHIN'

LET'S GO FISHIN' is a game where individuals try to collect as many fish as possible before their competition does. Even though it's seen as a classic children's game, the games found in this chapter can be used with all ages.

Game Summary

LET'S GO FISHIN' has a spinning game board with 21 plastic fish whose mouths open and close as the game spins around. The fish come in five different colors. There are four fishing poles included in the game. This game does require batteries.

Therapeutic Applications of LET'S GO FISHIN'

The game requires a steady hand and patience. Lessons gleaned from this game can include the need to be patient when trying to get something that doesn't come easy. Talking about outdoor activity options, such as fishing, that could improve one's lifestyle is another of the game's therapeutic lessons.

Discussion Prompts: Having patience when things don't come easily

1. Did you get frustrated at all when you didn't catch fish easily?
2. If you got frustrated, how did it make you feel physically? Does your body let you know when you're frustrated?
3. When things don't come quickly or easily in your own life, do you have the ability to be patient and wait, or do you become anxious?
4. Why is it important to be able to practice being patient?
5. What can you do to become more patient and less frustrated when things are taking longer than you'd like, or you find things to be difficult?

Discussion Prompts: Healthy activities to engage in outdoors

1. Is fishing something you have ever done? If so, what was the experience like for you?
2. What are your favorite activities to engage in outdoors?
3. Who do you like to do these activities with?
4. How can engaging in more outdoor activities, such as fishing, improve your life?
5. Are there any outdoor activities you haven't done but would like to try? If so, what steps can you take to make this happen?

LET'S GO FISHING' Games

Fishing Time

Objective
For group members to feel stress in a game situation to create the opportunity to discuss healthy ways to handle stress.

Who
People who experience a lot of stress in their lives and who need to discover healthy ways to handle this stress.

Group Size
2 or more

Materials
- LET'S GO FISHIN' game
- Stopwatch
- A prize the team can share (bag of candy, extra free time, etc.)

Description
Select an amount of time during which it would be difficult, but not impossible, for a member of your group to pull all of the fish out of the game. Next, announce the time to the group. Ask for a volunteer, or select one group member. Let them know that if they can complete the task in the time limit, then the entire group receives the prize you have selected. If the first person is unsuccessful, allow others to try.

Discussion Prompts
1. If you were the person who was fishing, how did you feel as you were playing the game? Did you feel pressure, stress, relaxed? Why?
2. If you didn't have the opportunity to go fishing, how did you feel when you were watching someone else try to win a prize for you?

3. What are the physical feelings you get when you feel stressed or anxious?
4. What are some ways you can deal with these feelings of stress when they occur?
5. Is it OK to feel stress or should you try to avoid it? Why?

Variation

➲ You may cut the time in half and have two people do this activity instead of just one.

Deep Sea Fishing

Objective
To provide a fun non-threatening environment that gives people the opportunity to answer questions about themselves at the level of deepness they're comfortable with.

Who
People who need encouragement to share and open up about themselves.

Group Size
2 to 8 is ideal

Materials
- LET'S GO FISHIN' game
- A copy of the *Fishing Chart*
- A copy of the *Question List* (found on following page)

Description
Before playing this game, show the group the Fishing Chart. Have everyone select the type of fish they would like to catch. Challenge group members to go for "deeper" fish if they feel up to the challenge of answering deeper questions or to catch "shallow" fish for more surfaced questions.

Allow everyone a turn to fish. After a player collects one fish, he or she must hand off the pole to someone else. Continue in this manner until all the fish are gathered. (Depending on your group size, some people may end up with more fish than others, but it should be as evenly spread out as possible.) After all the fish are caught, go around the group. Depending on the level of fish they caught, give each group member a question that reflects that level of sharing and opening up.

Discussion Prompts

1. Were you comfortable with the level of questions you had to answer?
2. Were you fishing for shallow or deep fish? Why?
3. Does it make you uncomfortable to answer deep questions? Why or why not?
4. Do you wish others would ask you more questions about yourself?
5. Are you someone that asks others questions? Why or why not?

Variations

➲ Using UNGAME cards, make piles of questions based on levels of deepness to go with each color.
➲ Only have three levels of fish and combine yellow/orange and green/blue.

Fishing Chart

Surface fish = Flying fish = yellow
Shallow fish = Dolphins = orange
Middle of the ocean fish = Viperfish = red
Deep fish = Lantern fish = green
Deepest fish = Giant squid = blue

Deep Sea Fishing List

Yellow: Surface fish
1. Favorite place to go out to eat
2. Favorite sport to watch
3. Favorite holiday
4. Favorite place to go for vacation
5. Favorite thing to do when you have free time at home

Orange: Shallow fish
1. What do you like to eat for breakfast?
2. What is your favorite time of day?
3. What do you most like to have conversations about?
4. What are your feelings about your hometown?
5. How do you feel about playing this game?

Red: Middle of the ocean fish
1. What is a talent you have that you're proud of?
2. What is something you wish you were better at?
3. Name something you like about your personality.
4. Name something you like about your appearance.
5. Name a goal you have for your life right now.

Green: Deep fish
1. Which member of your immediate family are you closest to, and why?
2. Which member in your extended family are you closest to, and why?
3. What team or group of people do you feel most a part of when you're with them?
4. What would your dream job be?
5. What accomplishment are you most proud of?

THERAPY GAMES

Blue: Deepest fish

1. What was the last thing you shed tears over?
2. Should you be trusted by others? Why or why not?
3. Who is the person in your life who understands you the most? Why?
4. Can your friends depend on you? Why or why not?
5. Describe a time when someone hurt your feelings.

Trait Fishing

Objective
For group members to share traits they're proud of with each other in order to build self-esteem.

Who
People who have trouble recognizing what their strengths and talents are.

Group Size
4 to 8 is ideal

Materials
- ⤳ LET'S GO FISHIN' game
- ⤳ Paper
- ⤳ Pens or pencils
- ⤳ Scissors

Description
Cut up 21 small slips of paper. Hand these out to group members (try to spread them out evenly among the group). Ask each person to write down a trait they have that they're proud of (something they're good at, have a talent for, etc.). They shouldn't put their name on these. Ask them to fold the slips of paper as small as possible; the paper will need to fit into the mouth of a fish from the game.

Fill the fish with the slips of paper so there is one per fish. Now play the game. If there aren't enough poles for each person, have them hand off their poles after each fish is caught. Allow time for everyone to catch at least one fish. After all the fish are caught, each person should pull the papers out of the fish they have. The group members then take turns reading these to the group. The person who caught the fish gets the first guess to try to figure out who wrote the trait. If they guess wrong, the rest of the group can guess until they figure out who wrote it. Award points to the person who guesses who wrote each trait.

Discussion Prompts

1. Was it easy or difficult for you to think of what your talents and strengths are?
2. Do you tend to focus on what you are good at or focus on what you are not good at more often?
3. What is negative self-talk? Do you engage in negative self-talk?
4. What is positive self-talk? Do you give yourself affirmations when you talk to yourself?
5. Can you think of strengths and talents you have that you did not list on your paper today?

Fish Guess

Objective

For group members to build self-esteem by receiving compliments from other group members.

Who

People who have low self-esteem and have trouble recognizing what their strengths and talents are.

Group Size

4 to 8 is ideal

Materials

➲ LET'S GO FISHIN' game
➲ Paper
➲ Pens or pencils
➲ Scissors

Description

Give group members a small slip of paper with someone else's name from the group on it. They should think of a compliment or something they admire about this person and write it down. They shouldn't put their name on the slip of paper. Have the group members fold each slip of paper as small as possible so it can fit into the mouth of a game fish. Place one slip of paper into each fish.

Play the game. If there aren't enough poles for each person, have players hand off their poles after each fish is caught. Allow enough time for everyone to catch at least one fish. After all the fish are caught, each person should pull the papers out of the fish they have. Group members take turns reading the compliments found in their fish to the group. The person the compliment is about tries to guess who wrote the compliment about them.

Discussion Prompts

1. How do you feel after hearing the positive things about yourself from someone else?
2. Do you often hear positive things from others? How does this affect you?
3. Why is it important to hear positive things from others?
4. How do you feel when you give compliments to others?
5. Do you always expect a compliment in return when you give one?
6. How can your life improve if you give or receive more compliments?

Variation

➲ If there are more fish than people, you can leave some fish empty or ask some group members to write more than one compliment.

Fishing for Compliments

Objective
For people to give and receive compliments in a non-threatening manner, in order to improve self-esteem.

Who
People with low self-esteem who could benefit from giving and receiving compliments.

Group Size
4 to 8 is ideal

Materials
➲ LET'S GO FISHIN' game
➲ A copy of the *Fishing for Compliments List*
➲ Scissors

Description
Make a copy of the *Fishing for Compliments List* (found on the following page), and cut each statement out so it's on a small strip of paper. Fold each of these statements as small as possible, and place one into the mouth of each fish from the game.

Play the game until all of the fish are pulled out. Each person should end up with a pile of fish at the end of the game. Have them pull the papers out of their fish (they can use a pencil or pen to flick it out if needed). Take turns going around the group opening up the pieces of paper to read, and then doing what it says.

Discussion Prompts

1. Were you more comfortable giving compliments to others, receiving them, or thinking of things about yourself? Why?
2. Did anything make you uncomfortable about this activity?
3. How often do you receive compliments?
4. How often do you give compliments to others?
5. Why is it important to hear compliments?

Variation

➲ If your group has more than four people, allow group members to hand off their fishing pole to someone who needs one after each fish is pulled out.

Fishing for Compliments List

Name something you're good at doing.

Ask a member of the group to tell you something you are good at doing.

What would you do as your talent if you entered a talent show?

Ask a member of the group to tell you what you should do at a talent show.

Give a compliment to the person on your right.

Give a compliment to the person on your left.

Give a compliment to the person who pulled out the least amount of fish.

Give a compliment to the person who pulled out the most fish.

Ask a member of the group to tell you what makes you a good friend.

Ask a member of the group to name a quality you possess that they wish they had for themselves.

Tell us why you admire someone who is in this group.

Tell the group one goal you have for yourself and why you know you'll be able to accomplish this.

Share a compliment you received from someone that you will always remember.

Tell the group what you think your best physical feature is.

Ask a member of the group to tell you what your best physical feature is.

Tell the group what you think your best personality trait is.

Ask a member of the group to tell you what your best personality trait is.

Tell the group the person in your life who makes you feel you're special and why.

Tell someone in the group why they're a good friend.

Tell someone in the group what their talent is.

What is the thing that people compliment you on the most?

IMAGINIFF

IMAGINIFF is a great game to play with group members or groups who are familiar with each other. Still, it can also be a lot of fun for a group of people who are new to each other. It's a game that reveals how others in your life see you. The game itself can really open up doors for discussion. The games found in this chapter don't require the IMAGINIFF game board but make use of the cards. This chapter provides a variety of ways for individuals to share how they see themselves and to learn how others view them as well.

Game Summary

IMAGINIFF comes with a set of question cards, a set of cards numbered 1 through 8, eight playing pieces, a game board, one grey playing piece, a dry erase marker, and an eraser. On the top of each card, there is a sentence with a blank in it. The blank will be filled in with a player's name. Below the sentence are six choices. The group will try to decide which choice the person on that card will choose. The numbered cards are used for voting purposes. The object of this game is to select the listed item you think a majority of the group will also select. This is how you earn points and advance on the game board. (Note: there are two versions of this game sold in stores. One version is from Buffalo Games and the other from Mattel. You can make either one work. The Buffalo version contains cards numbered 1-6 instead of 1-8. The Mattel version has additional cards). When using the Mattel version only the red cards are needed for the games in this chapter.

Therapeutic Application of IMAGINIFF

The game itself is an opportunity for individuals to learn how others view them. To offer even more therapeutic value, allow time at the end of each round for the person on the card to ask group members to explain why they made their choices.

Discussion Prompts: Self-discovery

1. Were you comfortable when the focus was on you or did this make you uncomfortable? Why?
2. Were you surprised by how others saw you?
3. How often do you get feedback from others on how you are as a friend, family member, teammate, etc.? Is it good to get this feedback or not?
4. What did you learn about yourself as a result of playing this game?
5. What did you learn about others as a result of playing this game?
6. What is the benefit of learning how others view you?

IMAGINIFF
Games

Guess Who?

Objective
For people to recognize how they perceive themselves and to be able to articulate this to others in a non-threatening manner.

Who
People who have trouble talking about how they view themselves.

Group Size
6 to 12 is ideal

Materials
- IMAGINIFF game cards
- Sticky Note strips (You can cut a sticky note pad into small strips if you don't have the small strips already.)
- Paper
- Pens

Description
Hand out three random game cards to each person, and give everyone three Sticky Note strips. Each player should look at their cards and put a strip next to the item on each card that they feel best describes them. Instruct the group to keep their individual piles of cards together, and not to let others see which cards belong to which person. Place the piles around the room and give each pile a unique number (you can use the number cards that come with the game for this or make your own if you need more). Give each person a piece of paper. Have them walk around the room, look at each pile, and try to guess which pile belongs to which individual. Award points for each correct answer.

Discussion Prompts

1. Were some people harder to guess than others? Why?
2. Were you really surprised by how any one player saw themselves?
3. Is it easier for you to identify character traits in others or in yourself? Why?
4. Did anyone select character traits for themselves that they would want to change?
5. What can you do to take steps towards making changes in your life?

Variations

- ➲ Allow people to turn in two cards for new ones if they don't relate to the cards they were given.
- ➲ Assign each person someone else. The other person must select the items that best fit the first player. Each person goes around the room, looks at each pile, and tries to determine which one was done about them.
- ➲ Have group members select how they think others view them, rather than how they view themselves.

Crack the Code

Objective
For people to share how they view themselves with others in a non-threatening manner.

Who
People who have difficulty sharing openly about themselves.

Group Size
4 to 10 is ideal (could be done in larger groups that are broken into smaller groups)

Materials
- ➲ IMAGINIFF game cards
- ➲ 3x5 cards (or paper)
- ➲ Pens

Description
Select four game cards that you feel will best reflect your group. Lay the cards out where everyone can see them. Make sure the cards stay in the same order so everyone knows which card is number 1, 2, 3, and 4. Give each person a 3x5 card and pen. Ask each group member to look at the cards and write down the number of the item that best fits them from each card and in the order of the cards. (It should be written in a code format 4-6-2-1.) Each person hands their code into the leader (have them write their name on it somewhere). The leader reads the codes out loud, and group members try to guess who wrote each code.

Discussion Prompts

1. Was it easy to select which items best represented you? Why or why not?
2. Was it easy to figure out which code belonged to which person? Why or why not?
3. Were you surprised by how some people saw themselves?
4. How well do you think the members of this group know you?
5. How well do you think you know yourself?

Variation

➲ Everyone draws the name of someone else and writes a code for that person. Then the leader collects the codes and reads them out loud. Each person has to guess which one was written about them.

Same or Different?

Objective

For people to recognize their desire to conform to what everyone else does, or their wish to stand out and be different. Also, to understand how this relates to one's self-esteem.

Who

People who have difficulty understanding what makes them unique and special. Also, those who are always trying to fit in by conforming to what everyone else does, or who try to be drastically different.

Group Size

4 to 12 is ideal

Materials

➲ IMAGINIFF game cards

Description

Select one game card that is a good fit for your group. Display it out so everyone can see. Give each person a set of the number cards that come with the game. (If you have more people than you have cards, you can use the first six numbered cards from regular decks of cards.)

Each person looks at the game card and selects the item that best fits them from the choices on the card. Everyone then selects the number card that goes with their selection; however, they don't reveal their number until the leader says to do so. At the same time, have everyone show the number of their selection. Award points to everyone who is in the majority (they selected the same number as a majority of the other group members). At first, individuals may be selecting what best fits them. However, in order to earn points, they may make their decisions based on what others do (this will lead to a good discussion on conformity and peer pressure). Play several rounds of this with a different card each time.

Halfway through the game, change the rules. This time, you can only earn a point if you're the only one who selects a specific number for each round.

Discussion Prompts

1. Did you select what best fit you or at times did you try to select what you thought everyone else would select in order to earn a point? Why?
2. Do you ever find yourself going along with what everyone else is doing in order to try to fit in, even if it means not staying true to yourself?
3. What is peer pressure? Do you ever feel peer pressure? How do you react?
4. When is peer pressure a bad thing?
5. Is it always a bad thing to go along with the group and to do what everyone else is doing? When is it not a bad thing?
6. Do you ever try to be so unique and different that others will notice you and you will stand out? Why or why not?
7. If you try to be different, are you staying true to who you really are or are you changing to be noticed?
8. Is it hard to stay true to who we really are?
9. How can you be yourself and still feel like you fit in?

How We View Others

Objective
To share with the group in a non-threatening manner how we view the people that we interact with the most.

Who
People who need to examine the roles that others play in their lives and how they view these individuals.

Group Size
1 or more

Materials
- ➲ IMAGINIFF game cards
- ➲ Paper
- ➲ Pens or pencils

Description
   Give everyone a piece of paper and a pen. Randomly select a game card (or pick a game card you feel will work best for your group). Announce who this card will be about (your mom, dad, sibling, grandparent, coach, boss, coworker, best friend, etc.). Ask each person to select from the card's six items the statement that best fits the selected person. On their paper, they should write down the sentence from the top of that game card, fill the person's name in the blank (mom, coach, friend, etc.), and then the words that go with what was selected. Select a new game card for each person they will be writing about. For at least one card, ask them to pick the item that best describes them. Allow time to share what was written down after the activity is complete.

Discussion Prompts

1. Do you tend to view other people in your life in a positive or negative light?
2. Do you ever have a life event occur that you won't let go of? As a result, do you always view someone with this event in mind, even though time has passed or things have changed?
3. Do you tend to view yourself in a positive or negative way? Why?
4. Is it healthy to only see the good in others?
5. Is it healthy to only see the bad in others?
6. How can you find the good in others but at the same time be aware of the negative influence someone may have in your life?
7. If there is someone in your life that is a negative influence, what can you do to make sure they don't influence you in a bad way?
8. Look at the names of people on your list who you know are a positive influence in your life. How can these people help you move forward when you need help?

Variation

➲ Ask group members to identify which specific item others would select to best describe them, rather than how they would describe these people.

If This Person?

Objective
For individuals to hear from others how they are perceived.

Who
People who would benefit from hearing how others perceive them.

Group Size
6 or more is ideal

Materials
➲ IMAGINIFF game cards

Description
Send one person out of the room. While they are away, select one person in the group to be "it." The person who left the room returns and tries to figure out who is "it" by selecting game cards and asking the question on the top of the card. The group members (including the person who is "it") shout out answers based on "its" personality. The person who is asking the questions may or may not give the group the list of items on the card to help them think of matches. After a while, the person who is doing the guessing tries to guess who was selected. After each round, allow the person who was "it" to ask individuals why they selected what they did to describe them.

Discussion Prompts
1. Did you like being the person who everyone was stating things about? Why or why not?
2. Were you surprised by what others said about you?
3. Do you think others know the real you or do they know only what you want them to know about you? Why?
4. Do you think you're observant about others and can accurately identify their traits, or is this difficult for you?
5. Why is it beneficial to be able to observe others and get to know who they really are?

Majority Wins

Objective
For people to learn how others view them.

Who
People who will benefit from learning how others view them.

Group Size
2 to 8 is ideal

Materials
➲ IMAGINIFF game cards
➲ Optional: Paper and pen to keep score, or beads to keep track of the score. Or prizes, such as candy or stickers.

Description
Have the group sit in a circle. Give each person a set of number cards with the numbers 1 to 6 on them. Use the number cards from the game. (If you need more, you can use the first six numbered cards from regular decks of cards.)

Select one person in the group to be "it" and lay down a card from the game. Everyone in the group must decide which number best fits this person (including the person who the card is about). At the same time, everyone reveals their card. If you're in the majority (you have selected the same number as most group members), you earn one point. If you laid down the same card as the person who is "it," you earn an additional point. Points may be calculated on paper, by handing out beads to keep track, or simply by giving candy or stickers instead of points. After each round, allow the person who is "it" to ask group members to share why they selected what they did. Do this for each person in the group.

Discussion Prompts
Discussion takes place after each round. At this point, the person who was "it" gets to ask the group why they made their selections.

THERAPY GAMES

BANANAGRAMS / SCRABBLE

The BANANAGRAMS game and the SCRABBLE game both contain a bag full of tiles with individual letters of the alphabet on them. Either of these games can be used for the activities in this chapter. The BANANAGRAMS game offers more letters but the SCRABBLE game has a point value on each tile. Although these two games are similar, they are opposite in the way they are played. The BANANAGRAMS game is very much an individual game with each person working independently from all others. In the SCRABBLE game people are building off of each other's work.

Game Summaries

The BANANAGRAMS game comes with a yellow fabric banana with a zipper. The banana is filled with 144 tile letters. To start the game, each person takes a set amount of letters (the number depends on how many players there are) and places these tiles face down on the table. On the go signal, everyone turns their tiles face up and works independently to use all of their letters to create a crosswords configuration of interlinking words. As soon as someone completes this challenge, they yell "peel," and everyone must take an additional letter. This continues until there are fewer letters in the banana than there are people. At this point, the first person to use all the letters in their possession to make a complete crossword wins the game.

The SCRABBLE game is a very popular game that is commonly found in the family game closet. The SCRABBLE game comes with 98 letter tiles, a game board, a bag for the letters, and tile holders to help display letters for each individual. Each player starts with seven tiles and places letters on the board to spell a word. The word must connect with a word that is already in place. The spaces on the board indicate if the word is worth more than just the point value on the tiles. After each turn, the word score total is tallied up and added to that individual's score.

Therapeutic Application of BANANAGRAMS

The game is very individual-based, with each person working independently from the others in their own space. The therapeutic discussion can be focused on the need to rely on our own skills and talents in order to move ahead in certain circumstances.

Therapeutic Application of the SCRABBLE game

In the SCRABBLE game the success of individuals is dependant on what others play on the game board and gives them a chance to work off of. Therapeutic discussion can focus on the need to rely on others at times in order to accomplish a task or be successful.

Discussion Prompts (BANANAGRAMS): Succeeding without any help from others

1. Did you enjoy working by yourself when playing this game?
2. Do you find yourself working independently in your life more often or do you like to get assistance from others when you work? Why?
3. If you find yourself in situations where you don't have any help from others and have to do everything on your own, do you feel stress or excitement about this situation?
4. If you have difficulty working by yourself but you find yourself in a situation where you can't rely on others, what can you do to make it easier for you to succeed?

Discussion Prompts (SCRABBLE): Relying on others

1. Were you able to determine what word you were going to play based solely on the letters you chose or did you have to wait to see what others played first?
2. Was it easier to find places to put words after there were lots of words on the board or when there weren't very many?
3. In your life, do you ever find yourself building off of what others have already done?
4. In your life, do you ever work by yourself on something but rely on others to do their part?
5. Is it a good or a bad thing to rely on others to help you?
6. What can you do to make it easier to accept help from others?

BANANAGRAMS

or

SCRABBLE

Games

Name Crossword

Objective
To increase self-esteem by recognizing positive traits in ourselves and in others.

Who
People who could benefit from hearing positive comments about themselves. Group members should be familiar with each other.

Group Size
4 to 10 is ideal (but you can break a larger group into smaller groups for this activity if you have extra games to get tiles from)

Materials
- ⊃ The BANANAGRAMS game or the SCRABBLE game
- ⊃ Optional: Camera

Description
Lay out all of the tiles face up. Select one member of the group to start with, and spell this person's name with the tiles in the middle of the table. The person's whose name is spelled out takes the first turn. He or she must create a word with the extra tiles in a crosswords format using one of the letters in his or her name to spell a positive trait they feel they have. (For example, if the name is AUSTIN, then he may use the tiles to spell the word ATHLETIC and intersecting it with the A, T, or I in his name). The next person must do the same but this time can connect to the word AUSTIN or ATHLETIC.

After each round, you may want to take a photo of the crossword that was created for the person it is about. They can keep the photo as a reminder of the positive traits others see in him or her. Start each round using the name of a different individual.

Discussion Prompts

1. Is it easier for you to think of positive traits for yourself or for others?
2. How do you feel about the words that were chosen to describe you?
3. Were you surprised by any of the words used to describe you? If so, why?
4. Did others have to give you ideas for the word you used to describe yourself?
5. Why is it oftentimes more difficult to think of positive traits for ourselves but not for others?

Variations

➲ Have the group divide into teams. Give each group a list of names of the members of one of the other teams. Each group has to create an individual "name crossword" for each member of the other group and then invite that person to look at it before starting another one.

Word Search

Objective
To recognize feelings we have when we feel left out of a group. To work together to include others.

Who
People who feel like an outsider. Also, people who aren't aware of how excluding others can hurt their feelings.

Group Size
12 or more

Materials
➲ The BANANAGRAMS game or the SCRABBLE game

Description
Give each person one letter tile. On the "go" signal, group members should move around looking for other letters they can combine with to form words. Award points to each person who is a part of a word (two points for a two-letter word, three points for a three-letter word, and so on). You may or may not write down the score. Anyone who hasn't found a word to connect with receives zero points for that round. Play a few rounds of this activity with the challenge of finding new words each time. You may wish to give each person a new tile after a few rounds to mix things up a bit.

Discussion Prompts
1. How did you feel when you weren't able to find a group that you could make a word with?
2. Did some letters make it harder to connect with others to create a word?

3. Do you usually feel like an X or an A in life (one that has trouble finding groups to connect with vs. one that doesn't)?
4. Have you ever found yourself in a situation where you were a part of a group and didn't include others on purpose? If so, how do you think those who were excluded felt?
5. What can you do the next time you find yourself in a situation where you see some people who are left out?
6. What can you do the next time you are in a situation where you feel left out?

Variation
➲ For smaller groups, you may want to give each person two tiles and they can choose to use one or both for this activity. However, the two tiles can only be included in one word at a time (not divided among two different words).

Word Challenge

Objective

For group members to work together in a fun, interactive, and competitive game to increase group interaction and social skills.

Who

People who could benefit from working together with others in a group setting.

Group Size

4 or more

Materials

- ➲ The BANANAGRAMS game or the SCRABBLE game
- ➲ Paper and pen to keep score with

Description

Divide the group into teams of two or more members each. A member from each team is selected to pull 20 random letters from the letter bag (without looking). After each team has collected their letters, call out a number. The challenge is to be the first team to make a complete word containing exactly that many letters. Points can be given for the amount of letters used in the word (a five-letter word challenge earns five points). You may do several rounds of this with a different number called out each time. Allow teams to change out their letters every so often.

Discussion Prompts

1. How well do you think your team did at working together?
2. Would it have been easier or more difficult for you to do this alone?
3. Did a leader emerge in your group? Was this helpful?

4. What role do you usually take on when working in a group setting?
5. Do you like the role you take on or do you wish you could be more of a leader, more of an equal team member, or more of a follower?
6. What are the benefits of being able to work with others to accomplish a task?
7. Can you name some times in your life when you have to work with others?
8. What can you do to improve your ability to work in a group with others?

Variations

➲ Remove the difficult letters (X, Q, Z, etc.) prior to both teams selecting their letters from the bag.
➲ At the end of the challenge, allow time for each team to race to be the first team to make a crossword-like arrangement out of their entire pile of letters.

Building Words

Objective
To discover how the choices we make as individuals can affect others.

Who
People who need to think about the choices they're making in their own lives.

Group Size
4 or more

Materials
- The BANANAGRAMS game or the SCRABBLE game
- Paper
- Pens

Description
Divide the group into teams of two to eight members each. One at a time, each team member will go to where you have a pile of letter tiles laid out and select a specific number of tiles. (You want each team to end up with a total of around 20 tiles.) When selecting the tiles, allow individuals to look at the letters. However, don't allow them to let the others in their group know what was chosen until everyone has selected their tiles. Once everyone has collected their tiles, team members reveal the letters they chose to their own team and put them all into one pile.

Set a time limit (three to five minutes), and challenge the teams to use their letters to make as many words as possible by rearranging them. Have them write down the words on their paper. You may give points according to how many words they come up with, extra points for longer words, etc. The team with the most points at the end wins.

Discussion Prompts

1. Did the letters you chose make it easier or harder for the group to create words?
2. Did you have control over what letters your team members chose?
3. If you chose your letters after they had been picked through, how was your selection compared to others?
4. In your own life, do you ever experience times when the choices you make have an affect on a group of people?
5. Do you find the choices you make in life usually help or hurt others?
6. Do you feel like you have control over the choices you make?
7. Do you ever feel like the choices others make hurt you?
8. If others make poor choices that affect you, how can you overcome this obstacle?

Variations

- After each team has made as many words as they can with their letters, have them write the words down on a list. Send the list and letters to another group, who can get bonus points for any additional words they make.
- Let people collectively choose which letters to use. Next, either allow them to keep the letters or make them trade with another group.

Lucky Letters

Objective
For group members to recognize the positive traits that exist in each other.

Who
People who could benefit from hearing positive comments about themselves. Group members should be familiar with each other.

Group Size
4 to 20 participants

Materials
- The BANANAGRAMS game or the SCRABBLE game
- Paper
- Pens or pencils
- A timer or stopwatch

Description
Divide the group into two even teams. Ask each team to write down all the names of the people on their team and on the other team onto one piece of paper. Once all the names are written down, randomly select a letter of the alphabet from the pile of letter tiles (you may wish to take the difficult letters out, such as Z, Q, etc.). Inform the teams what letter was chosen, and give them two minutes to work as a team to think of a positive word, or words, beginning with the chosen letter that describes each person. For example, if the letter H was chosen and the names Emily, Taylor, and Jacob were on the list, a team may come up with: (1) Emily: Hard worker; (2) Taylor: Honest, Humble; and (3) Jacob: Handsome.

Once the time limit is up, bring the two teams together. Ask them to each read their list to the group. For added fun and competition, you may give each team a point for every word on their list that isn't on the other team's list.

Play as many rounds of this game as you have time for. You may want to make specific rules for the activity (i.e., you must think of at least one word for each person on the list). The Discussion Prompts may be used at the end of each round or wait until the end of the entire game.

Discussion Prompts

1. How do you feel about the words that were chosen to describe you?
2. Were you surprised by any of the words used to describe you? If so, why?
3. Did anyone write down a word for you that is also a word that you would use to describe yourself?
4. Is it easy or hard to think of positive words to describe others? Yourself? Why?

Variations

➲ Don't give a time limit; instead, give points to the team that thinks of a word to describe everyone on the list first.

➲ With a large group, don't include your own team on your list. Instead, just think of words to describe the members of the other team.

Scrambled

Objective
To think about the attributes a person needs in order to overcome the hard times and adversity they may find in their lives.

Who
People who struggle to find the inner strength to overcome hardship.

Group Size
1 or more

Materials
⊃ The BANANAGRAMS game or the SCRABBLE game
⊃ A copy of the *Scrambled Words List*

Description
Select the letters for one of the words found on the *Scrambled Word List* (or think of words that would better fit for your group). Lay the letters out in a scrambled fashion where everyone can see. The words represent attributes a person should have in order to overcome the adversity they may face in their life. You may give clues if the group is having a hard time guessing what the word is. The first person to guess the word earns a point.

After someone guesses the word, ask the group to discuss its definition. Have the group talk about how it can be used to help them face the difficulties they encounter in their own lives.

Discussion Prompts
1. Of all the words we used today, which one do you think you have the most of?
2. Which one do you wish you had more of? Why?
3. How can you build up your _____ (fill in the blank with different words from the list)?

Variation

➲ Play in teams. Whoever guesses the word first earns a point for his or her team.

Scrambled Word List

Courage
Strength
Teamwork
Ambition
Friendly
Honesty
Bravery
Desire
Hope
Spirited

Love Letters

Objective
For group members to recognize positive traits that exist in each other and in themselves.

Who
Individuals who could benefit from hearing positive compliments from others and finding things that are positive about themselves.

Group Size
2 to 12 is ideal

Materials
➲ The BANANAGRAMS game or the SCRABBLE game

Description
Pass the bag of letters around so individuals can take turns pulling out one letter each. They earn one point if they can think of a compliment for another member of the group that starts with that letter. If they can also think of some way to give themselves a genuine compliment with a word that starts with that letter, then they earn an additional point. (You may or may not allow descriptive words to be used such as "amazing singer" for the letter A, even though the second word does not start with an A.) The individual with the most points at the end can be declared the winner. (Having a winner is just to make the game more entertaining, and points should be awarded in a fun manner. You may even give out random amounts of points that nobody even keeps track of for fun.)

Discussion Prompts
1. Was it easier to give or receive compliments? Why?
2. Was it easier to think of nice things about others or about yourself? Why?
3. Do you feel uncomfortable when others give you compliments?
4. What did you learn about yourself as a result of this game?

Team Spelling Bee

Objective
For a team to work together to problem-solve and to accomplish a task.

Who
People who need to work on social skills when working with others.

Group Size
12 or more

Materials
➲ The BANANAGRAMS game or the SCRABBLE game

Description
Divide the group into two or more equal teams of six to eight members each. Give each team an equal number of letter tiles (try to divide the letters as equally as you can between the teams).

To play the game, the leader says a category (i.e., a wild animal), or asks a question, and the answer must be spelled out. The group members must decide on a word to spell using the tiles they have (e.g., lion, tiger, hyena). They must quickly decide who will be holding which letter (one letter per person) and run up to the leader where they line up in the order to spell the word for the leader. Award one point to the team who spells a word first and one bonus point to the team who creates the word containing the most letters. If a team can spell a word with more letters than they have people, then the team members can hold two letters for that word.

Discussion Prompts
1. What was harder, agreeing on a word to spell or actually spelling the word as a group?
2. Did anyone emerge as a leader in your group?
3. What role did you take on for your team? Leader, follower, helpful participant, etc.?
4. Do you like your role or is this something you wish to change?

THERAPY GAMES

RORY'S STORY CUBES

RORY'S STORY CUBES is a game that is simple and easy to use. The game is all about using your imagination to tell stories based on the pictures that appear on the cubes when they are rolled randomly. The cubes offer different ways for individuals to be creative when they play the game or when they think of new ways to use these unique cubes. The game itself is compact and easy to take with you wherever you go.

If you don't have this game, you can have your group create your own unique nine story cubes (see *Create Your Own* in this chapter).

Game Summary

RORY'S STORY CUBES come in a small compact box. There are nine cubes and on each side a different item is pictured. The game instructions give three game options. These include rolling the cubes and telling a story using the nine images that roll to the top, telling a story that relates to a theme, and each person telling a different part of a story based on the cube they end up with.

You can also find RORY'S STORY CUBES – Action Edition with pictures of action words appearing on each cube. These can be combined with the original or used separately. RORY'S STORY CUBES – Voyages is another version offered with pictures of things you would more likely find in a far-off land. You can even find the story cubes as an App for your phone or iPad.

Therapeutic Application of RORY'S STORY CUBES

When using the simple version of the game, a player rolls the cubes and tells a creative story. Or the group can look at the cubes and each person writes a story. Through the game, we can discover what types of things individuals may be focused on, thinking about, or have experiences with.

Discussion Prompts: Self-discovery

1. What do you think the story you told tells us about you?

2. Where you able to discover anything about someone else in the group by listening to their story?
3. Who in the group would you say has a skill for telling stories?
4. Are you more comfortable writing your stories or telling them out loud? Why?
5. Is it easier for you to tell a fictional story than it is to tell a real story about yourself? Why or why not?
6. How can you use fictional stories as a way to cope with something that is difficult?

Discussion Prompts: Self-esteem
1. Why is it that each person can look at the same pictures and come up with a completely different story?
2. What would the world be like if everyone had the same thoughts, ideas, and way of seeing things?
3. Each person is unique and different from every other person. What qualities do you possess that makes you special and sets you apart from others?
4. Do we tend to embrace our differences or do we try to blend in and be like everyone else?
5. How can you benefit from embracing the things that make you different from others?

Discussion Prompts: Communication skills
1. Did you find it easier to be the one telling the story or listening to others tell a story?
2. When you're listening to someone tell a story, what's going on inside your head? Are you picturing the story, thinking about how you would tell the story differently, thinking of the story you will be telling, or thinking about something else completely?
3. Is this how you usually are during a conversation when someone is sharing something with you?
4. When you were the one telling the story, how could you tell if others were listening to you?
5. How can you show someone you are listening to them? Why is this important to do?

RORY'S STORY CUBES Games

Fortune Teller

Objective
For an individual to think about their future and what would be the best choices to make and goals to set for themselves.

Who
People who would benefit from being encouraged to set positive goals for themselves.

Group Size
4 to 12 is ideal

Materials
> ○ RORY'S STORY CUBES

Description
Place the cubes in a bag (or other container), and have individuals take turns pulling out three cubes from the bag and rolling them. When the three pictures come up, the individual tells the group what his or her own "fortune" is by creating a positive story about what will happen to them based on the pictures. Continue in this manner and give each group member a chance to share.

Discussion Prompts
1. Do you feel that you have control over your own future or does it feel like it is up to the fates as to how it will turn out?
2. Do you think you have the power to change the course of your life even if it feels like the future is already set in stone for you?
3. What steps can you take to ensure a positive future for yourself?
4. What can you do if it feels like life is moving in a positive direction and all of the sudden you have something happen that turns your life upside down? Can you ever get back on track again?
5. Have you ever written goals for your own future? If so, how did it help you? If not, do you think it can help you?

Variations

➲ The "fortune" can be negative, funny, or positive. This allows for the opportunity to see how the individual sees his or her own future and makes for interesting discussion time.

➲ Do more than one round of this. The first time, ask each person to say a negative fortune, and the second time, a positive one. Find out which one came easier for the individuals.

➲ Ask group members to be fortune tellers for their neighbor and to create a fortune for the person sitting next to them.

Cube Questions

Objective
To express yourself in a creative way and to share about your life with others in the group.

Who
People who have trouble sharing their thoughts and feelings with others and who need a means of expressing themselves verbally.

Group Size
4 to 12 is ideal (but the game can be done with 1 person, or with a larger group than 12)

Materials
⮞ RORY'S STORY CUBES
⮞ A copy of a list of statements with words missing for a "fill in the blank" activity

Description
   Roll all nine cubes onto the table or floor where everyone will be able to see. Read a statement with a blank in it (see list below for ideas). Each person must select an item from the cubes that most represents how they view themselves in relation to the statement. Encourage group members to think abstractly by picking items that represent something in their lives. Allow time for sharing for each statement. Continue doing this but mix up the cubes, so you are using different ones every time.

My mood right now _____
My family _____
My future _____
The place I live _____
The way I spend my free time _____
My friends _____
How my friends see me _____

Discussion Prompts

1. Was it difficult for you to find things on the cubes to fill in the blanks? If so, do you think it's possible that you have trouble thinking abstractly or that you're not sure of how you see your own life?
2. If you could make up a cube of your own, what would you put on it to help you fill in the blanks?
3. What did you learn about someone else in the group as a result of this exercise?
4. What did you learn about yourself as a result of this exercise?

Cube for You

Objective
To learn how others perceive us, so that we may come to a better understanding of who we are.

Who
Group members who are familiar with one another and who could benefit from hearing how others perceive them.

Group Size
4 to 9 is ideal

Materials
➲ RORY'S STORY CUBES

Description
The group sits in a circle and each person is given one cube. Select one person to roll his or her cube, and then he or she looks at the picture that comes up on the top. Next, this individual decides which member of the group this picture most represents and shares with the group who they chose and why. Continue in this manner around the circle until everyone has had a chance to share. (It's possible that everyone may not be chosen by a group member. However, this can be a good thing to discuss at the end of the activity.)

Discussion Prompts
1. How did you feel about what others said about you when they chose a cube that represented you?
2. If you didn't get chosen by anyone, how did this make you feel? Why do you think you didn't get chosen?
3. Do you think you see yourself the same way others see you?

4. How do you think others see you? Do you ever wish they saw you differently?
5. What can you do to change the perception that others have of you (if this is something you desire)?

Variation

➲ If you have more than nine members in your group, give a cube to nine members who are sitting by each other. After each person has used his or her cube, have them give it to the first person in the circle who doesn't have a cube. Rotate the cubes around the group.

Who Filled in the Blank?

Objective
To learn how others view us to gain a better understanding of ourselves.

Who
People who would benefit from receiving feedback from others to gain a better understanding of how they come across.

Group Size
6 or more

Materials
- RORY'S STORY CUBES
- Paper
- Pens or pencils

Description
Select one person to leave the room. After they leave, select one of the remaining group members to be "it." With the exception of the person who left the room, everyone thinks about the person who is "it" and looks at the cubes to find one thing that they feel represents that person. Each person is given a small piece of paper, and he or she writes down the sentence from below and fills in the blank as it pertains to the person who is "it." The leader collects the papers and calls the person who left back into the room. The leader then reads the sentences out loud, and the person tries to guess which member of the group they are talking about in the notes. Once the person guesses correctly, the person who was "it" can ask people to clarify why they wrote what they wrote. Afterwards, move on to the next round.

This person is like _____ because _____ .

Discussion Prompts

1. What did you learn about yourself as a result of this activity?
2. What did you learn about others in the group?
3. Is it hard for you to figure out how you're feeling?
4. Is it easy or difficult for you to share how you're truly feeling with others? Why?

Variation

⮕ Play in teams. Each team selects one person to be "it" on their own team, and then writes up clues about this person using the "fill in the blank" sentence. When the two teams come together, they each try to guess which member from the other team the clues are about.

Cube Clues

Objective
For people to give and receive positive comments as a way of improving their self-esteem.

Who
People with low self-esteem who could benefit from hearing positive comments about themselves. Also, those who need practice giving positive comments to others.

Group Size
3 to 10 is ideal

Materials
➲ RORY'S STORY CUBES
➲ Paper
➲ Pens

Description
Select one person to leave the room. Give each of the remaining members one of the cubes, a pen, and a piece of paper. Ask each person to look at their cube, select one of the cube's pictures, and write a sentence about the person who left the room using that picture as a word in the sentence. The sentences should be positive in nature and reflect the good qualities of the person.

After everyone has finished writing their sentences, the leader collects them and brings the person back into the room. The leader reads one of the sentences and asks the person who had been out of the room to guess who wrote it. If he or she guesses correctly, he or she earns one point. Read two or three more before giving someone else a chance to leave the room. After each round, give the person the pieces of paper that others wrote about them to keep as a reminder of their good qualities.

Discussion Prompts

1. How difficult was it to make a sentence out of what you had on your cube?
2. Is it easier or harder for you to think of positive comments about yourself or about others?
3. How well do you feel the others in the group know you if you were one of the people who left the room?

Line Up

Objective
For group members to work together to create a story and to learn more about one another in the process. For individuals to practice communicating with others.

Who
A group of people who could benefit from working together, learning more about one another, and practicing communication skills.

Group Size
4 to 9 is ideal

Materials
➲ RORY'S STORY CUBES

Description
Randomly give each person one of the story cubes and ask them to hang on to it. Ask the group to line up in various ways (e.g., from tallest to shortest, oldest to youngest, by birthday month, longest hair to shortest, etc.). Once the group has lined up, ask each person to select one side of their cube and place it face up in their hand. The person at the front of the line starts telling a story that contains what is on his or her cube, and each person in the line then adds to the story until the last person wraps it up. Do several rounds of this with a different lineup category each time.

Discussion Prompts
1. Which activity required more communication skills, lining up or the story time? Why?
2. Did someone take the lead when you were lining up or did everyone participate equally in figuring out where everyone should go?

3. When you were the one telling the story, did you feel that people were listening and interested in your story? What clues did you use to figure this out?
4. Did you enjoy telling the story more or listening to the other stories more?
5. Who in this group has a gift for telling stories?
6. Did you learn anything about anyone in the group during the lineup part of the activity?

Variations

➲ Individuals don't reveal which side of the cube they want to use until it's their turn and based on the story so far.
➲ One person walks down the line and tells a complete story adding whatever each person has face up in their palm.

Deserted Island

Objective
To use teamwork to make decisions and create a group story.

Who
People who could benefit from practicing working with others on a group project in a situation that requires teamwork.

Group Size
1 or more

Materials
- ⊃ RORY'S STORY CUBES
- ⊃ Optional: Paper and pens

Description
Tell the group they are stranded on a desert island and must figure out as a team how it is they will get off the isle. However, they will only have a few items they can use. Roll the nine cubes. The objects that appear are the objects that the group can use to get themselves off of the deserted island. They must create a story that contains all of the items and share it with the leader.

Discussion Prompts
1. Was it easy or difficult to make decisions as a group? Why or why not?
2. Did anyone in the group emerge as a leader? Was a leader needed?
3. Can a group function without a leader?
4. What role did you find yourself in for this activity? Leader, follower, contributor?
5. Would you have preferred to do this alone? Why or why not?
6. Do you find yourself wishing you could work alone more often or do you wish you could work with others more often?
7. What social skills do you need in order to work with others in a group setting?

Variations

➲ Divide the group into two teams and give each team four cubes. Each team comes up with their own scenario based on the four items that appear on their cubes.

➲ Divide the group into more than one team and roll all nine cubes. Each team must create their own unique story as to how they can escape the island using all of the items. This can also be done with each individual creating their own story.

➲ Roll the cubes and allow each team to select three of the items to use.

What Do You Remember?

Objective
To recognize the importance of paying attention to detail and remember what we hear and see in order to improve communication skills.

Who
People who have difficulty remembering what they hear and see because of their inability to focus.

Group Size
1 or more

Materials
- ➲ RORY'S STORY CUBES
- ➲ Paper
- ➲ Pens or pencils
- ➲ Plate or tray

Description
Roll the cubes and place them on a plate or tray to display them in a manner that everyone in the group can see. Give 20 seconds for group members to look at the cubes and try to memorize what's showing on the top side. Take the cubes away and hand out paper and pens. Challenge each person to remember what was on the cubes and to write these items down. After everyone has created a list, bring the cubes back and hold them up one at a time. Award points to anyone who had that item on their list. You can do several rounds of this but roll the cubes each time to mix them up.

Discussion Prompts

1. Why might it be important to have the ability to remember what we see and hear?
2. Were there some objects on the cubes that were easier for you to remember than others? Why?
3. Are there some things in our lives that hold special meaning so we can remember those things more easily?
4. What types of information do you tend to easily remember?
5. What types of information do you tend to easily forget?
6. How will your communication skills improve if you improve your ability to remember what you see and hear?
7. What can you do to help yourself remember details better than you do now?

Variation

⮑ Take the cubes away and engage the group in a conversation for a minute about anything. After the brief discussion, ask them to write down what was on the cubes.

Quick Change

Objective
To recognize the importance of being able to stay focused and pay attention to detail when communicating with others.

Who
People who are easily distracted and who have difficulty staying focused.

Group Size
1 or more

Materials
➲ RORY'S STORY CUBES

Description
Gather the group around a table or spot on the floor. Roll the nine cubes where everyone can see them. Give the group 20 seconds to look at the cubes and to try to memorize what they see. After the 20 seconds, have everyone close their eyes or turn around so they can't see the cubes while you take one cube away. Give a signal for everyone to look at the cubes. The first person to say which cube was taken away earns a point. Play several rounds of this game and roll the nine cubes each time.

Discussion Prompts
1. Why is observation an important part of the communication process?
2. Do you ever miss important details because you were not being observant or paying close attention?
3. How can your ability to communicate be improved if you work on having better focus and paying more attention to details?
4. What can you do to improve your ability to pay attention to details?

5. How can you show someone you're listening and focused on what they are saying?
6. How do you feel when you know someone is focused on what you're saying?

Variations

➲ When taking a cube away, move the remaining cubes to make it more challenging to observe what's missing.

➲ Instead of taking a cube away, turn one so it has a different object showing and the group must guess which object is new.

Create Your Own

Objective
To open up the minds of group members to the possibility of creating their own games or planning their own unique activities. This could be done instead of going along with the unhealthy activities they're engaging in.

Who
People who engage in unhealthy activities during their free time and could benefit from exploring new ways of doing things.

Group Size
1 or more

Materials
⮥ Paper
⮥ Pens, pencils, or markers
⮥ Tape or glue
⮥ RORY'S STORY CUBES (optional)

Description
Show the group the RORY'S STORY CUBES game. Let them know that they will be making their own story cubes. (Or if you don't have the game, this is an opportunity to create your own.)

Make a blank copy of the cube pattern (found on the following page) for each group member and hand them out. Ask group members to create their own story cube by drawing a simple picture on each side of the square. Each picture should show one item or action.

Play one of the games in this chapter using your own story cubes that have been created by the group.

Discussion Prompts

1. Did you like the fact that we created our own story cubes rather than using the ones that you could buy?
2. How often do you not do an activity because you don't think you have the right equipment but really you could improvise and come up with a different way of doing the same activity? Can you think of an example of when you have done this or of something you could do?
3. Are there activities you engage in that are emotionally or physically unhealthy for you? Can you think of ways to turn those activities into healthy activities?
4. Did you find the creative process more fun when creating your own story cubes or when using them for a game?
5. Is there an activity you enjoy that brings out your creativity that might replace some of the destructive and negative activities you might be involved in?

Variations

⮂ Each picture should be of a face making a different expression. The stories should be about a person and the different emotions they are feeling.
⮂ Each picture can be of an activity group members could engage in during their free time. These should be healthy alternatives to their current destructive behavior.

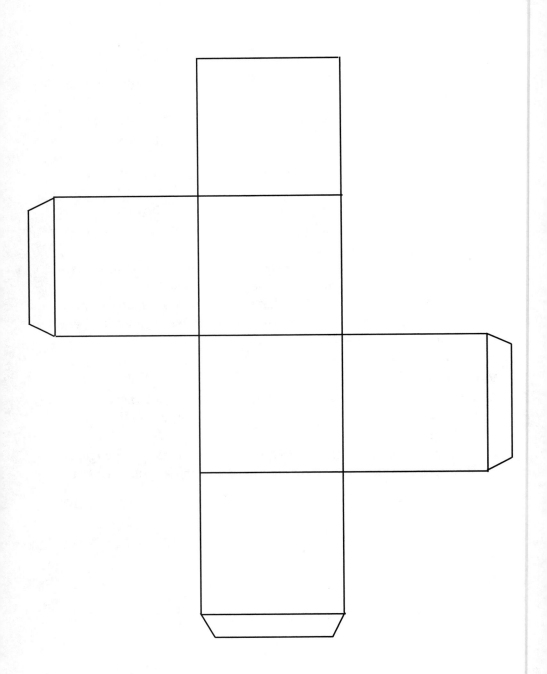

THERAPY GAMES

OPERATION

The OPERATION game is a classic kid's game. However, it can also be used for older groups with the games found in this chapter.

Game Summary

The OPERATION game comes with a game board that has a picture of a man on it. "Cavity Sam" has holes in his body where different playing pieces are placed which correspond with that part of the body. The man's nose is a red light bulb that buzzes when the tweezers that are used to pull out a game piece touches the side walls of the hole where the game piece was found. In some editions of the game, cards are used to determine which piece a player needs to pull out, and money is earned for successfully completing an operation.

Therapeutic Application of The OPERATION game

The OPERATION game can be very frustrating at times since it requires a steady hand and patience. This can lead to a good discussion about dealing with frustration in one's life.

Discussion Prompts: Dealing with frustration

1. Do you find this game to be frustrating at all?
2. Do you feel symptoms of stress when playing this game? If so, what symptoms do you feel?
3. How do you feel when you're watching others try to pull out a piece?
4. How do you usually deal with a situation that you find to be frustrating?
5. What are things you can do to better deal with a frustrating situation?

THERAPY GAMES

OPERATION
Games

Match Up

Objective
To explore ways to deal with feelings, emotions, and tough situations in life.

Who
People who could benefit from exploring ways to deal with difficult situations, by talking about activities that can serve as coping skills.

Group Size
1 to 8 is ideal

Materials
- The OPERATION game
- A copy of the *Match Up List*

Description
The leader selects one activity from the *Match Up List* and reads it to the group (without reading which game piece goes with that activity). One member of the group tries to guess which game piece matches the activity and attempts to pull it out. If the correct piece is successfully pulled out, then that person earns $100 from the game. If the incorrect piece is pulled, it must go back into the game. The next person attempts to find the right piece.

Discussion Prompts
1. Which activity on the list would you most likely use to deal with a difficult situation? Which one would you least likely use?
2. How often do you handle a situation in a negative way? How can you change this?
3. What are other ways you can handle a difficult situation?
4. What is the advantage of realizing the coping skills that could benefit you *before* you're in a negative situation?

Variation

⭢ Ask group members to create the list themselves of what activities each game piece represents.

Match Up List

Do a crossword puzzle or read a good book. *Brain Freeze*

Talk with a friend. *Adam's Apple*

Ask someone for forgiveness and give forgiveness to others. *Broken Heart*

Set goals for your future. *Wish Bone*

Watch a show that makes you laugh. *Funny Bone*

Try a new restaurant with a friend. *Spare Ribs*

Do something outside of your comfort zone. *Butterflies in Stomach*

Write about it. *Writer's Cramp*

Try a new recipe. *Bread Basket*

Spend time with your pet. *Charlie Horse*

Take a nice relaxing bath. *Water on the Knee*

Fix something that is broken or clean something that is disorganized. *Wrenched Ankle*

Exercise your muscles. *Anklebone Connected to the Knee Bone*

Take and Talk

Objective
To encourage people to share their thoughts and feelings with the group in a non-threatening manner.

Who
People who have difficulty talking about themselves.

Group Size
2 to 8 is ideal

Materials
➲ The OPERATION game

Description
Draw a card from "Doctor" pile to find out what item has to be pulled out of the body. If successful at getting the item out, then the person gets a chance to answer the question that corresponds with the piece pulled out. If they answer the question honestly, they get the amount of the money on the card. If they choose to pass and not answer the question, they put the piece back inside the man. This player can try for another question on their next turn.

Discussion Prompts
1. What did you learn today that you didn't already know about someone?
2. Do you feel uncomfortable answering questions about yourself or do you like the chance to share with others? Why?

Variation
➲ If you pull out the piece, you get to ask someone in the group the question that corresponds to the piece selected.

Brain Freeze: How can you use your intelligence to improve your life?

Adam's Apple: What ways can you use your voice to help yourself or others?

Broken Heart: Is there someone in your life you need to ask for forgiveness? How will this help you?

Wish Bone: What is one wish you have for your future?

Funny Bone: What makes you laugh? Why is laughter good for you?

Spare Ribs: Do you have anything in your life that you can spare and share with others?

Butterflies in Stomach: What makes you nervous? How can you get control of your nerves when you're nervous?

Writer's Cramp: How can writing down your feelings help you?

Bread Basket: What blessings in your life are you thankful for?

Charlie Horse: Tell us about an animal that has been special in your life.

Water on the Knee: What items would you put in your bucket if you were running out of your house during a fire?

Wrenched Ankle: Where can you walk when you feel like you need some time to yourself?

Anklebone Connected to the Knee Bone: What exercises do you find to be most therapeutic for you?

Fast and Frantic

Objective
To work under pressure and to show that you can handle the stress the group may be feeling.

Who
People who feel overwhelmed when feeling pressured to get everything done.

Group Size
2 to 8 is ideal

Materials
- The OPERATION game
- Stopwatch
- Prize for the group (This can be tangible or something intangible like extra free time.)

Description
Tell the group you're going to see how fast they can work together to get all the pieces out of the OPERATION game without making the nose light up. Group members should take turns attempting to pull out any piece they wish while the leader times the group with a stopwatch.

After all the pieces are out, offer a prize to the group (anything you know the group would be excited about, such as candy, free time to play games, etc.) if they can pull out all the pieces in a faster time than they just did. If they don't make it in a faster time, you may give them several tries.

Discussion Prompts
1. How did you feel the first time you played this game and you knew it was being timed?
2. How did you feel when there was a time to beat in order to win the prize?

3. Did you feel stress at all when everyone was rushing you to beat the time when it was your turn?
4. Do you ever feel stress when facing pressure to get things done in your own life?
5. How do you manifest stress when you feel it?
6. How do you deal with stress when you feel it?
7. What's the best way for you to deal with stress in your life?

Variation

➲ If the group is unsuccessful in beating their time, then they owe the leader something such as cleaning up, singing a silly song, etc.

Self-Compliment

Objective
To find positive traits and qualities in ourselves and to share these with the group in a non-threatening manner.

Who
People with poor self-esteem who could benefit from finding positive traits in themselves.

Group Size
4 or more

Materials
- The OPERATION game
- Paper
- Pens or pencils

Description
Give each person a very small piece of paper (about ½" x 2"). Ask them to write down something they like about themselves and to not share with others what they have written. You can be specific and ask them to note one of their talents, what quality makes them a good friend, etc.

After each person has written down their self-compliment, collect the notes and fold them into small pieces that can fit into the OPERATION game slots (remove the game pieces prior to this). Allow group members to take turns trying to pull out any of the self-compliments. If they pull one out successfully, they earn a $100; if they can also guess who wrote the compliment, they earn an additional $100. If they guess wrong, then the self-compliment goes back into the game for another person to pull it out and guess.

The person with the most money at the end may win the prize of being put on the "hot seat." That means the others will say what it is they admire about this person.

Discussion Prompts

1. Was it difficult for you to think of a compliment for yourself? Why or why not?
2. How often do you have negative thoughts about yourself? How often do you have positive thoughts? Why is important to know the difference between these two types of thoughts?
3. How can it benefit you to take the time to find your own positive traits?
4. How can you build on the positive traits you have to become a better person?

Variation

➲ If you have more than 13 people in your group, you may have some self-compliments that are extra. As compliments are successfully pulled out, an extra self-compliment can be used to fill the vacant spot.

Out of Place

Objective
To explore ways to deal with difficult life situations. Also, to find appropriate ways to put one's life back together when it feels like it has fallen apart.

Who
People who need to explore ways to deal with difficult situations.

Group Size
1 to 10 is ideal

Materials
➲ The OPERATION game

Description
Prior to the group time, mix up the pieces so each piece is in the wrong slot (minus the rubber band). The list found here will help you find a space each piece can fit into fairly well. Challenge the group to put the game "back together" by taking turns pulling out pieces and putting them into the correct space. You may offer the group a prize as an added incentive for completing this task, or just present the game as a fun challenge.

Discussion Prompts
1. Do you ever feel that you need to be "put back together" by your friends or family members after you have fallen apart or gone though a difficult time?
2. Do you ever feel that things in your life are out of order?
3. When you feel that things are out of place or like you need to be put back together, who do you turn to for help?

4. Why is it that we need to rely on others to help us put our lives back together sometimes? Is it OK to rely on others?
5. Would you say your life is falling into place right now or are you in need of help from others in order to put your life back together? If you need help, are you asking for it?

Place the first piece into the second slot…
Writer's Cramp to Spare Ribs
Spare Ribs to Wrenched Ankle
Wrenched Ankle to Writer's Cramp
Wish Bone to Butterflies in Stomach
Butterflies in Stomach to Bread Basket
Bread Basket to Broken Heart
Broken Heart to Adam's Apple
Adam's Apple to Funny Bone
Funny Bone to Charlie Horse
Charlie Horse to Water on the Knee
Water on the Knee to Brain Freeze
Brain Freeze to Anklebone (This one may be sticking out a bit.)

TABOO

The TABOO game is great for a wide variety of ages, fun for families to play. It's very interactive and fun. The new ways to play the TABOO game that are found in this chapter focus mainly on communication skills and the need for good listening skills. Also, there's an element of imagination that is used to stimulate creative thinking.

Game Summary

The TABOO game is played with two teams competing against each other to guess the words on the top of cards. Each card has a main word on the top and then five additional words listed below. One team member gives clues to his or her teammates trying to get them to say the word on the top of the card. However, the person who is giving clues isn't allowed to use any of the words listed on the card. A member of the opposing team looks over the clue-giver's shoulder to make sure none of the listed words are used. This person has a buzzer, ready to buzz when the clue-giver says a forbidden word. After the time has run out, award points for each word they were able to guess correctly. This continues back and forth between the two teams until a predetermined score is reached.

Therapeutic Applications of the TABOO game

The focus of this game can easily be on communication skills. Each participant needs to listen carefully to what is said by the clue-giver, without being distracted by all the yelling coming from others who are calling out words. The clue-giver must articulate clearly and think of clear ways to communicate without using the specific words and without getting flustered.

The TABOO game can also be used as an object lesson to talk about feeling left out. It's a game that certain people seem to dominate because they yell louder than others, while some people have a mind that is focused on guessing words. Those who have a quiet voice or who don't think as quickly may sit back and let their teammates play while they just observe or tune out.

Discussion Prompts: Focus and listening skills

1. Was it easy or hard for you to focus on the person who was giving clues? Why?
2. Did it help to hear what your teammates were guessing? Why?
3. Did you find it distracting to have everyone yelling guesses at the same time?
4. Are you easily distracted when you're talking with someone? If so, how does this make the process of communication difficult for you?
5. When you were the one giving clues, how could you determine if your team was clearly understanding what you were saying?
6. How did you know your teammates were focused on what clues you were giving?
7. What are the things we can do to show others we are focused and listening to what it is they're saying?
8. What are some things you can do to improve your ability to focus and listen to others?

Discussion Prompts: Feeling left out

1. Did you notice how some people in this game dominated the guessing?
2. Did anyone guess right but the clue-giver didn't hear it, so your team kept on guessing?
3. If you weren't heard, was it because your voice is quiet? Or were others being more assertive with shouting out their answers?
4. Has anyone had an experience where they were a part of a group but felt unheard and/or not noticed?
5. How do you feel when you feel that you're in the background and are going unnoticed?
6. Is there anyone who would like to change from being a background person to someone who is engaged with the group?
7. What are some positive things you can do to assure you're not always in the background?
8. If you're someone who is often the center of attention, how can you help others who are feeling left out and in the background?

TABOO
Games

Story Clues

Objective
To play a communication game requiring individuals to listen carefully to determine the clues in the story.

Who
People who have trouble sharing their feelings directly and who hope others can pick up on hints and clues.

Group Size
2 or more

Materials
➲ The TABOO game
➲ Paper
➲ Pens or pencils

Description
Give each person a piece of paper and a pen. One person in the group selects a card and must tell a short story using all the words on it. (You may wish to set a time limit for this story.) Group members attempt to guess the six words by writing down six guesses as the story is told. After the story, have the storyteller read the words on their card. Each person earns a point for every correct word they have on their list.

Discussion Prompts
1. What clues did you listen for to help determine what the words were?
2. What listening skills did you have to use today to pick up on the clues?

3. Do you tend to tell people how you feel directly? Or do you let them guess how you're feeling through the clues you give to them?
4. What happens when you think someone got your clues but it turns out they didn't at all?
5. In what circumstances would it help you to be more direct, rather than relying on clues?

Fill in the Blank

Objective
To discuss ways we communicate with clues, hoping others pick up on them, rather than stating our feelings clearly.

Who
People who have trouble effectively communicating with others.

Group Size
2 or more

Materials
➲ The TABOO game
➲ Paper
➲ Pens or pencils

Description
Give each person a piece of paper, pen, and one TABOO game card. Allow two minutes for everyone to write a story that contains the words on their card. (The words should appear in the story in the same order as on the card.) Each word from the card should actually be left out of the written story and instead a blank line is drawn in that spot.

After everyone has completed their story, ask each person to switch papers with someone else. The group members silently read the story they were given, and they guess at each missing word by filling in the blanks. Each person then reads their story to the person who wrote it. Points are awarded for each word they guess correctly.

Discussion Prompts
1. What did you do to help the person who read your story have a better chance of figuring out the correct words?
2. Was it easy for you to figure out the words? Why or why not?

3. Do you ever give clues and hope others will fill in the blanks, rather than stating your true feelings?
4. Why do we sometimes give clues, rather than clearly expressing our feelings and thoughts?
5. Do you ever have conversations with someone who isn't direct and gives clues?
6. Does this kind of communication work?
7. How can it benefit your life to improve your ability to communicate with others?

Reverse

Objective
To focus on the importance of using good listening skills when communicating with others.

Who
People who often get distracted when others are talking and who need to practice using good listening skills.

Group Size
2 or more

Materials
- The TABOO game
- Paper and pen for keeping score

Description
Divide the group into two teams. The setup is the same as for The TABOO game, with teams taking turns sending one team member up front with a stack of cards in the card holder. Once the timer is set, the person with the cards reads the word at the top of the first card. Their team earns a point when a teammate shouts out one of the listed words on the card. Then the person moves on to the next card. Continue until the timer runs out and count the points earned for that round. Play several rounds of this game, giving different group members a chance to call out the words.

Discussion Prompts
1. When you heard a word, how did you select a word to shout out?
2. Did you notice how different people have different associations with different words?
3. As the person up front with the words, did you give your team clues somehow? Or did you just wait for them to figure it out?

4. What did you need to do when listening in order to be successful in this game?
5. What was your mind focused on when playing this game?
6. Do you ever get distracted when you're listening to someone talking?
7. How can you show someone you're tuned in and listening to them?
8. Why is it important to have good listening skills?
9. When do you need to use your listening skills the most?

Variations

➲ For smaller groups, the leader calls out the word. The first team to come up with a word on the card earns a point.

➲ Assign point values to the words on the card. If the first word is shouted out, then the team earns five points, second word equals four points, and so on.

Moment of Memory

Objective
To practice focusing, listening, and remembering what is said.

Who
People who have difficulty staying focused when listening. Those who often forget what others say because they have trouble paying attention.

Group Size
2 or more

Materials
- The TABOO game
- Paper
- Pens or pencils

Description
Give everyone a piece of paper and pen. Tell the group that they can't start writing until you say "go." Select one of the game cards and read all six words on the card to the group. After reading the words, give the "go" signal. Everyone tries to remember the words and writes them down to earn points. Do several rounds of this using a new card each time.

Discussion Prompts
1. Was it easy or difficult for you to remember what the words were?
2. What did you do to help yourself remember?
3. Do you ever have trouble remembering conversations you have with people?
4. Do you ever forget important information?

5. What can you do to improve your ability to remember what you hear?
6. Why is it important to be able to focus and remember what someone else is saying to you?

Variation

⮑ After reading the words, have the group do something before giving them a chance to write down the words (20 jumping jacks, walk around the room, answer a math question, etc.).

What Is the Word?

Objective
To focus on the importance of using good communication skills when listening to others.

Who
People who need to work on improving their listening and observation skills.

Group Size
2 to 20 is ideal

Materials
⮕ The TABOO game

Description
Divide the group into two teams. Select one card from the TABOO game. Read one of the words found below the main word for that card, and give each team a chance to guess what the main word is. This can be done in a "shout out" fashion, or by team members taking turns making a guess. If nobody guesses the main word, read another word from the card. Continue in this manner until one team guesses the main word, or all the words are read. If neither team guesses correctly, you may give additional clues until either team is successful. Do several rounds of this game, awarding points to each team as they guess the words correctly.

Discussion Prompts
1. What did you have to do during this game to figure out the word?
2. Do you think the leader was able to tell who was focused and paying attention and who wasn't? If so, how?
3. Do you think you are someone who can easily focus and pay attention?

4. Why is it important to be able to focus when others are talking to you?
5. What are some things that distract you when someone is talking to you?
6. What happens when you don't focus and miss some of the information?
7. Have you ever been in a conversation with someone where you felt like you were only getting part of the information they were trying to convey?
8. If you only get part of the information, is this because you have trouble focusing or because they had trouble communicating?
9. How can you make sure you understand if you feel that you only received part of the information?

Variation

➲ Each team selects a team member to pick a card. That person then reads the words to their own team to try to get them to guess the main word. The opposing team gets to guess if the first team doesn't figure out the main word after hearing all the supporting words.

THERAPY GAMES

CHUTES AND LADDERS

CHUTES AND LADDERS is a popular game. Most people have played it at one time or another, either as a child or with a child. Even though it is thought of as a child's game, it can be used in therapy for older ages too. Playing the CHUTES AND LADDERS game is a fun way to look at the consequences of our actions.

Game Summary

The CHUTES AND LADDERS game comes with a game board, four playing pieces and a spinner with the numbers 1 through 6 on it. Players move along the board, and when landing at the bottom of a ladder, they get to skip spaces and go all the way to the top of the ladder. When landing at the top of a chute, the player must slide down and move backwards on the board to the bottom of the chute. The first one to arrive at the top of the game wins.

At the top of each chute, there is a picture of an action that the character on the board is going to do, and at the bottom of the chute, there is the consequence of doing it. At the bottom of each ladder, there is a good deed or accomplishment a character will be engaged in, and at the top of the ladder, there is the reward or outcome of the good deed.

Therapeutic Application of the CHUTES AND LADDERS game

The negative and positive results that come from our own actions are exemplified in this game of going forward for doing good things and moving backwards for doing negative things. This creates an opportunity to discuss the good and bad things we do in life and the consequences that come from our actions.

Discussion Prompts: Positive Coping Skills

1. In your life, do you feel like you slide backwards or move forward more often? Why?

2. When you feel like your life is going backwards, what are some things you can do to avoid sliding back any farther?
3. When you feel like your life is going backwards, what can you do to make it move forward?
4. What are some things you can do to keep from finding yourself in a situation that causes you to slide down?

Discussion Prompts: Anger Management
1. Did it frustrate you to move ahead in the game only to find yourself in a situation where you slid backwards?
2. Do you ever slide backwards in your own life by exploding when you become angry?
3. In this game, you had to go back down the chute when there was a negative action. What are some ways you have handled your anger negatively that have caused you to slide backwards?
4. Have you ever been able to control your anger when you could feel yourself about to explode? What did you do to keep from exploding and what was the outcome?
5. Why is it important to think of ways to deal with your anger before you find yourself in a situation that makes you angry?

CHUTES AND LADDERS Games

Consequences and Rewards

Objective
To explore actions we take in our lives that are negative and to understand the consequences that can occur. To explore positive things we can do and understand the rewards for choosing a positive way to live instead of a negative one.

Who
Individuals who would benefit from looking at positive ways to deal with situations and understanding the consequences of acting in a negative manner.

Group Size
4 to 10 is ideal (find items to use as game pieces if you have more than four)

Materials
- The CHUTES AND LADDERS game
- 2"x1.5" Sticky Notes (or regular size Sticky Notes and cut them into smaller sizes)
- Scissors, if needed
- Pens or colored markers
- Extra game pieces (if you have more than four players)

Description
   Hand out four small Sticky Notes to each person. Ask everyone to create two new spaces for the game that can be associated with one negative thing that a person might do to slide backwards in life. The first Note tells of the action and the second one reveals the consequence. These can be just words on the Note, or they can draw pictures. Ask each person to do the same thing regarding a positive behavior, with one positive action listed on one Note and the reward revealed on the other.

   Ask the group members to share what they have come up with.

Then place the negative ones on a chute and the positive ones on a ladder before playing the game as a group. When a person lands on a related space, ask them to share with the group any time they may have had a similar experience.

Discussion Prompts

1. Was it easier to think of situations that held negative consequences or positive rewards? Why?
2. Do you think about the possible outcomes before you act? Or do you act first and then worry about the consequences later?
3. Was there any positive action that someone put on their Sticky Note that you would like to do more often in your own life?

Variations

- ⮑ Use paper instead of Sticky Notes and cut the paper into pieces the size of a space on the game board.
- ⮑ Ask group members to come up with enough cards to fill all of the CHUTES AND LADDERS game spots on the board (hand out more than four notes to each person).
- ⮑ Have the group think of the new spaces for the board as a group and the leader writes them down.
- ⮑ Make a paper copy of the game. Next, have each person fill in blank Notes for CHUTES AND LADDERS negative and positive actions and consequences as described above. Share with the group about the new game board they have created.
- ⮑ After creating the new spaces, play the game but do not place the Sticky Notes on the game until someone lands on a chute or a ladder. At that time, they can share what they came up with.

Honest Answers

Objective
To encourage self-discovery by creating a fun way for individuals to answer questions about their own thoughts and views.

Who
People who have difficulty sharing openly about themselves to others.

Group Size
4 to 10 is ideal (find items to use as game pieces if you have more than four)

Materials
- The CHUTES AND LADDERS game
- List of questions (See list with this game, or use a book of questions, use questions from another game such as The UNGAME. See *Variations* for other options.)

Description
Prior to playing the CHUTES AND LADDERS game, create a list of questions that participants must answer about themselves. Anytime someone finds themselves at the bottom of a ladder, they can choose to answer a question in order to move up the ladder or they can stay put and choose not to answer a question. When a player lands at the top of a chute, they can answer a question to keep from sliding down the chute or choose not to answer a question and go down the chute. The first one to the top wins; however, in order to win, the player must first answer a question.

Discussion Prompts
1. Do you like to answer questions about yourself? Why or why not?
2. How do you feel when you share openly and honestly about yourself?

3. What did you learn about someone else in the group that you didn't already know?
4. How can you learn about others?
5. Why is it good to ask others about themselves?

Variations

➲ Create a question list that better reflects the members of your group.

➲ The questions can be selected randomly, or go down the list to the next question, or give each person a choice of which question to answer from the list.

➲ Instead of using a list of questions, someone in the group can ask a question to the person that they must answer.

➲ Prior to the activity, have the group come up with the list of questions that are to be used for the game. Write the questions on cards that are placed in a draw pile to be used while playing.

Question List

1. What makes you sad?
2. What makes you feel loved?
3. What would you do if you were to perform in a talent show?
4. Who is your favorite extended family member? Why?
5. What was the last thing you had an argument with someone about?
6. What is the favorite gift you ever received? Why?
7. What qualities do you have that make you a good friend to others?
8. Can you remember a time when someone made fun of you? How did you feel?
9. If you could trade places with someone for a day, who would it be and why?
10. What is something you have regrets about doing?

Positive Pile

Objective
To discover the benefits of having more positive activities, events, and influences in one's life than negative.

Who
Individuals who could benefit from discussing the need for having more positive influences in their life than negative ones.

Group Size
4 to 10 is ideal (find items to use as game pieces if you have more than four)

Materials
- The CHUTES AND LADDERS game
- 2 bowls
- Marbles or rocks or beads (or simply use two different colors of paper cut into small squares) in two different colors

Description
Gather a pile of beads, rocks or marbles and put them in two bowls (mark one "Up" and one "Down"). Each bowl should contain items of one color (or each can be unique in some other way from the other bowl, such as containing items of the same shape). Play the CHUTES AND LADDERS game. Each time a player goes up a ladder, he or she selects an item from the "Up" bowl. When going down a chute, they select an item from the "Down" bowl. At the end of the game, the person who has collected more "Up" items than "Down" items is declared the winner. Emphasize the benefits of having more positive experiences than negative to live a healthy balanced life.

Discussion Prompts

1. In a typical day in your own life, would you collect more "Up" items or "Down" ones?
2. What can you do to add more "Up" events in your own life than "Down" ones?
3. Do you create your own events or do you simply react to what others do?
4. How can you take more control of adding positive and getting rid of negative in your own life?

Variations

➲ Don't move up or down the ladders. Just move around the board and collect marbles as you land on the proper space.
➲ Only give items for going up ladders and skip giving out the down items.
➲ At the end, one "Up" marble equals one positive point and one "Down" marble equals one negative point. Figure out point value based on this formula.

Safety

Objective
To discuss ways to deal with situations where individuals do not feel safe or feel threatened by another individual.

Who
People who could use new coping skills to deal with unsafe situations they find themselves in.

Group Size
4 to 10 is ideal (find items to use as game pieces if you have more than four)

Materials
- The CHUTES AND LADDERS game
- Blank 3x5 index cards
- Pens

Description
Hand out 3x5 index cards to group members. Ask them to write down situations they have found themselves in where they didn't feel safe or felt uncomfortable. These can be situations where they were not using proper safety equipment (e.g., not wearing a seat belt in a car or not using a bike helmet when on a bike), or situations where they don't feel safe due to feeling threatened by another individual (e.g., a classmate threatened to beat them up after school or offered them drugs). Each card should have only one situation listed on it. Place all of the cards into a pile.

Now play the CHUTES AND LADDERS game. Each time someone finds themselves at the bottom of a ladder or the top of a chute, they can choose a card. They then share with the group how they would handle the unsafe situation in order to go up the ladder or to avoid going down the chute.

Discussion Prompts

1. Did you relate to very many of the unsafe situations that were found on the cards?
2. After hearing what others wrote, did you think of anything else you could have added but didn't think of when writing the cards?
3. Did you hear any good ways to deal with tough situations that you hadn't thought of before?
4. Does the same way of dealing with a difficult issue apply to every situation? Why or why not?

Variation

➔ The leader creates the cards of unsafe situations prior to playing the game.

Ups and Downs

Objective
For people to recognize ways they handle their anger poorly and to find ways to handle their anger in a productive manner.

Who
People who have issues with the way they deal with anger.

Group Size
4 to 10 is ideal (find items to use as game pieces if you have more than four)

Materials
- The CHUTES AND LADDERS game
- 3x5 index cards or paper
- Pens or pencils

Description
Hand out ten 3x5 index cards to each person. Ask participants to write down ways they handle their anger that are effective (or ways they should handle their anger) on half of the cards, with one way per card. On the remaining cards, players write down ways they have handled their anger in the past that are negative or destructive behaviors, with one per card.

Play the CHUTES AND LADDERS game. Whenever a player gets the opportunity to go up a ladder, he or she must share one of their positive cards with the group. When a player reaches the top of a chute and has to go down, he or she must share a negative way they have handled anger in the past. At the end of the game, allow participants to read all of their cards aloud which were not used during the course of the game.

Discussion Prompts

1. Did it frustrate you to move ahead in the game only to find yourself in a situation where you slid backwards?
2. Do you ever slide backwards in your own life by exploding when you become angry?
3. When you heard the negative ways that others have handled their anger, were you reminded of ways you have handled your own anger that had negative consequences?
4. In this game, you had to go back down the chute when you handled your anger in a negative way. What are the negative consequences in your life of dealing with your anger in a negative way?
5. Did you learn anything from listening to what others would do to handle their anger in a positive way?
6. Have you ever been able to control your anger when you could feel yourself about to explode? What did you do to keep from exploding and what was the outcome?
7. Why is it important to think of ways to deal with your anger *before* you find yourself in a situation that makes you angry?

Variations

- Instead of using 3x5 index cards, simply give each person a piece of paper. Ask them to make a list of ways they handle anger in an effective way and another list of ways they have handled their anger in a negative manner. Have them share something from their list when landing on an "Up" or "Down" space.
- After sharing a negative way of handling anger, a player doesn't have to go down the chute if he or she shares what could have been done differently.
- Mix all the cards up in a pile. Each person draws one card from the pile to read, and he or she has to decide if it is a good or a bad way to handle anger before moving on.

THERAPY GAMES

PUZZLES

A simple 24-piece puzzle can be used for all the games found in this chapter. Puzzles are something almost everyone can do, and I have found that working on a puzzle with others creates an opportunity for group interaction and discussion time. People can talk and engage with one another without feeling uncomfortable with silence because the puzzle is the focus, not the conversation.

Depending on the size of your group and the functioning level, you may choose to use puzzles with more pieces.

Therapeutic Applications of Puzzles

Puzzles can be something people can use to fill their time when they feel alone. They supply a pastime that can be chosen instead of engaging in a harmful or unhealthy activity. Puzzles can also be used as a tool to form a bond with someone through an easy conversation over the work of putting a puzzle together.

Discussion Prompts: Coping skills
1. How often do you take the time to put together a puzzle?
2. Do you find you're more relaxed when you work on a puzzle?
3. If you're more relaxed when working on a puzzle, how can you use puzzles or other similar activities to help yourself cope with difficult situations in your life?
4. Is this an activity you would more likely do alone or with others?
5. How can it help you in your own life to take the time to do an activity that you do just for the entertainment value?
6. When you have free time on your hands, what do you usually fill it with?
7. Are some of the things you fill your time with unhealthy for you?
8. If you fill your life with unhealthy activities, what activities could you do instead?

THERAPY GAMES

PUZZLE
Games

Puzzle Positive

Objective
To create lists of positive and negative words that can be used to describe people. Also, to compare the differences it can have in our lives to hear positive words instead of negative ones.

Who
Individuals whose self-esteem is easily damaged by hearing negative words. People who use negative words to hurt others.

Group Size
2 to 24

Materials
➲ One 24-piece puzzle
➲ Paper and pen or pencil for each person

Description
Use a 24-piece jigsaw puzzle, and write one number on the back of each piece using the numbers 1 through 24. Put the puzzle together prior to the group meeting (or have the group put it together at the start of the group time).

Once the puzzle is put together, give each group member a piece of paper and pen or pencil. Group members take turns selecting a piece of the puzzle and removing it from the puzzle. They then look at the number on the bottom side. The number will correlate with a letter of the alphabet (1=A, 2=B, 3=C, etc.), with the exceptions of Y and Z. Once everyone has selected a piece, ask them to write down the letter that corresponds with the number on their piece. Give them the challenge of writing down as many words as they can think of that can be used to describe people that start with that letter. These can be positive or negative words. For example, if the letter is A, then the words could be Awesome, Athletic, Antsy, Active, Adventurer, Artistic, Awful, etc.

After everyone has completed their lists, ask them to circle all the positive words and cross out all the negative words. Then everyone counts their positive words and adds up their negative words. They figure out how many more positive words they had than negative (if they have more negative ones, they should come up with a negative number). You can declare the person with the biggest number as the "winner," or keep it non-competitive and simply ask people to share what they came up with.

Discussion Prompts

1. Did you have more positive words or negative ones? Why was it easier for you to think of these kinds of words?
2. Do you hear more positive or negative words in your life? How does this affect you?
3. Do you give more compliments or more put-downs? How does this affect you? How does it affect others?
4. If you need to hear more positive comments, is there anything you can do to create this in your life?
5. If you need to cut down on the negative comments you say, is there anything you can do to change this?
6. What are four words that you can find circled on any list created today that describe you?
7. What are two words you can find circled that you don't think currently describe you but you'd like to describe you someday?

Variations

⊃ Do this as a group rather than individually, and think of words together to create a big list.

Missing Pieces

Objective
To discover what people feel is missing in their own lives, and to figure out what they're doing to try to fill the void.

Who
People who are always trying to fill a void they feel with something that may not be healthy.

Group Size
1 or more

Materials
⊃   Any size puzzle that your group can put together in one session.

Description
Select a puzzle for your group to put together. Prior to the group time, hide as many pieces as there are people in your group around the meeting room. Don't tell the group there are pieces missing. Simply have them all work together to put together the puzzle. Once the puzzle is put together (minus all the missing pieces), use the Discussion Prompts for the 1st session.

After the discussion time, let the group know about the pieces that are hidden around the room. Each person needs to find one piece in order for the puzzle to be complete. After everyone has found one piece, ask them to identify things that they can change in their own life to make their life whole again. As each person speaks, they can put their piece into the puzzle. When the puzzle is complete, move on to the Discussion Prompts for the 2nd session.

Discussion Prompts – 1st session
1. Can you relate to a puzzle that has missing pieces in any way?
2. What is something you always feel like you're missing and searching for?

3. Is this a healthy or negative thing for you to spend your time searching for? Why?
4. If you feel like there's a void in your life, what do fill this void with? Is this negative or healthy?
5. Do you think some people focus too much on what they feel is missing and they overlook all the good they have?

Discussion Prompts – 2nd session
1. Can you relate to a complete puzzle that is all put together in any way?
2. When do you feel that your life is whole and complete?
3. If you're someone who is always searching for something, what can you do to make your life whole?
4. What is something you can change in your life *right now* to fill in the holes and make yourself whole?

What Is It?

Objective
To discover how we can hurt others when we only know a part of a person's life story but make judgments based on the small part we know. To discuss ways to keep from being hurt by the judgment of others who only know a part of our life story.

Who
People who often use gossip to hurt others or who are often hurt by the gossip of their peers.

Group Size
1 to 12 is ideal

Materials
➲   One 24-piece to 100-piece puzzle

Description
    Select a puzzle that is 24 to 100 pieces (more for larger or more advanced groups, less for lower functioning or smaller groups). Place all of the pieces in a bag that is not "see through." Don't let the group know what the picture is on the puzzle. Group members take turns selecting one piece at a time from the bag and taking a guess as to what the picture will be when the puzzle is complete. After each guess, the piece is laid out where everyone can see. As pieces are pulled out of the bag, allow any group member to put pieces together that they can connect. Once someone guesses what the complete picture is, give the group the remaining pieces and allow time for them to complete the puzzle.

Discussion Prompts

1. How difficult was it to know what was on the puzzle during the first round of picking pieces?
2. How were you finally able to figure out what the picture was?
3. Have you ever experienced a situation where someone only had a little bit of information but they thought they knew the whole story?
4. Have you experienced gossip that was about someone (or about you), where someone only had a small piece of information but thought they knew the whole story and told others?
5. When we only know a part of someone else's story, how can we keep from hurting them?
6. If others only know a small part of our own story, how can it hurt or help us to fill in the other pieces of the puzzle?

Observation

Objective
To understand the importance of observation and focus when a person is asked to pay attention to details.

Who
People who are easily distracted and who have difficulty focusing on the details and therefore miss out on receiving important information.

Group Size
2 to 8

Materials
➲ One 24-piece puzzle (You may select a puzzle with more pieces for a more advanced group.)

Description
Select one puzzle piece and lay it out in the middle of where the group meets, so everyone can see it. Lay out the remaining puzzle pieces on a table that is away from the group.

Divide the group into two or more teams of two to four members each. Pick one person to go to the second table to select a piece they think will connect to the piece in the middle of group. The person's team will receive one point, if the selected piece can lock into the existing piece. If not, the piece must go back to the table and no points are awarded. Continue in this manner, giving different individuals a chance to select a piece for his or her team until the entire puzzle is completed.

Discussion Prompts

1. Which of your communication skills did you have to use in order to select the right piece?
2. Is communication always done through listening or is observation an important tool too?
3. What type of information can you acquire through observation that you don't always get from just listening?
4. What kinds of cues can you give to others to communicate with them by using your actions and body language?
5. Do you think others can tell when you aren't focused or listening? If so, how?
6. How do you feel you do at observing the details?
7. What can you do to improve your ability to observe details?

Variations

➲ Do as one group rather than as teams. However, give the group a time limit to try to get the puzzle completed.

➲ Do with more than one puzzle and with more than one team. The teams compete against each other to finish their own puzzle first.

Physical Puzzle

Objective
To engage in a fun fitness game to encourage exercise and to explore ways physical exercise can benefit individuals both physically and mentally.

Who
People who could benefit from understanding how putting exercise into their routine will benefit them emotionally and physically.

Group Size
1 or more

Materials
➲ One 24-piece puzzle
➲ A copy of the *Physical Puzzle Exercise List* found on the following page

Description
   Use a 24-piece jigsaw puzzle, and write one number on the back of each piece using the numbers 1 through 24. Place the pieces into a box, or pile, and pull one piece out at a time. Read the number on the back, and look at the list to find which exercise goes with that number. When all the group members complete the exercise, then the group earns that piece. You can offer some sort of reward for the group to earn for completing the puzzle (extra free time, a snack, etc.).

Discussion Prompts
1. How were you feeling emotionally and physically before we started this activity?
2. How do you feel emotionally and physically now?
3. How often do you get exercise?
4. How can exercising regularly benefit you emotionally?
5. How can improving your fitness level benefit you?

6. What are some ways you like to work out?
7. What can you do to add more exercise to your daily routine?

Variations

➲ Have individuals earn pieces for the group by selecting a piece and completing the exercise.

➲ This can be made into a fun relay race between two teams by using two puzzles. Each team tries to complete their puzzle first, by doing exercises to earn pieces, and then by working as a team to put the puzzle together.

➲ You can use a 100-piece puzzle. Leave some pieces blank or use each number more than once on the back of the puzzle pieces.

➲ This activity can be done a little at a time, whenever you need to get your group up and moving for just a few minutes.

Physical Puzzle Exercise List

1. 3 Push-ups
2. 8 Sit-ups
3. 15 Jumping Jacks
4. Give everyone a "high 5"
5. Hop up and down on each foot ten times
6. 5 Squats and back up
7. 10 Leg lifts with each leg while sitting in a chair
8. Run in place for the count of 20
9. Do a crazy dance for the count of 20
10. Walk quickly around the perimeter of the room four times
11. Jump up and reach as high as you can 20 times
12. 10 Frog hops (Hop like a frog in place)
13. 6 Push-ups
14. 12 Sit-ups
15. 20 Jumping Jacks
16. Hop up and down on each foot 20 times
17. 8 Frog hops (Hop like a frog in place)
18. Run in place for the count of 30
19. 7 Squats and back up
20. Walk quickly around the perimeter of the room six times
21. 8 Leg lifts with each leg while sitting in a chair
22. Jump as high as you can 15 times.
23. Touch your toes eight times
24. Do any exercise of your choice for the count of 30

CARDS AND DICE

Decks of cards and dice are inexpensive, easy to find, and can be used almost anywhere. The games in this chapter make unique use of these simple game supplies to create games that provoke discussion about a variety of topics.

Game Summary
The games in this chapter use ordinary decks of cards and dice. Some games may require more than one deck or more than one pair of dice.

Therapeutic Applications of Cards and Dice
Card games can be taught as an inexpensive activity that group members can engage in with friends and family as a form of appropriate social interaction.

Discussion Prompts: Social interaction with others
1. When playing a card game, do you simply play the game or is there group interaction that is taking place at the same time?
2. What type of group interaction is taking place?
3. Can you learn more about another person by playing cards with them? Why or why not?
4. How often do you play card games with your friends and family?
5. What are your favorite card games to play and why?
6. Would you like to learn more card games? If so, how can you go about this?

THERAPY GAMES

CARDS AND DICE Games

Royal Zap

Objective

For group members to recognize things that make them unique and to give each other compliments to improve self-esteem.

Who

People with low self-esteem who could benefit from hearing and accepting compliments from others and who need to recognize their own unique qualities. Group members should be familiar with one another.

Group Size

4 or more

Materials

- ➲ 1 deck of cards
- ➲ Paper and pens or pencils

Description

Prior to this activity, have everyone write their name on the top of a piece of paper. Place these pieces of paper on a table with a pen or pencil somewhere in the room, but away from the group.

Sort through a deck of cards and use only the 2, 3, 4, and face cards (king, queen, jack) from each suit. Decks of cards may be combined to make a bigger pile of these select cards.

Gather the group in a circle. The first person selects a card from the pile. Whatever number the card says, the person who selected the card must say that many facts about themselves (things they like, what they do for fun, places they have lived, their talents, etc.). If the person draws a face card, they get "zapped." This means that they must go to the paper pile and start writing down compliments on the pieces of paper belonging to the other group members. The zapped group member must continue writing compliments until someone else gets zapped and takes their place. After the game is complete, hand out the papers and allow time for everyone to read them.

Discussion Prompts

1. Was it easier to say things about yourself or to write down the compliments for others?
2. What did you learn about someone else in the group that you didn't know already?
3. How did it feel to read what others wrote about you?

Variation

➲ Stack the papers with the names on them, and have the individuals each write a compliment on the top paper. Next, place it on the bottom of the pile before moving on to the next one. This will ensure everyone will get close to the same amount of compliments on their paper.

Group Card Tower

Objective
To work together to accomplish a difficult task.

Who
People who need to practice working with others to improve social skills.

Group Size
2 or more

Materials
➲   1 deck of playing cards per team

Description
   Divide the group into smaller groups of two to four people each, giving each group one deck of cards. Instruct the groups that their task is to build the highest tower of cards they can. When building the tower, each person may use only one hand and must place the other hand behind his or her back. The teams must start over each time the cards fall. It's a good idea to set a time limit for this activity. See which team has the tallest tower once the time is up.

Discussion Prompts
1.   What was needed from you and your team members to accomplish this task?
2.   Was anyone frustrated at any time during the activity? If so, how was it handled?
3.   How important would your teammates' help have been if you all could have used two hands?

4. Do you ever find yourself needing help from others because you have something missing (good hearing, good eyesight, full use of arms or legs, strength, etc.)? If so, how do you feel about asking others for help?
5. Do you have anyone in your life that needs your help? Do you offer it?

Variations

➲ Start with both hands, then halfway through switch to one hand and compare the difference.

➲ Use your dominant hand part of the time and your other hand part of the time, and then compare the two.

Something New to Do

Objective

To practice social skills by teaching each other new games to play and by listening and following directions. For individuals to learn new activities they can engage in with others that are healthy ways to spend free time.

Who

People who need to practice speaking in front of a group and those who need to practice listening skills. People who need to learn new healthy activities they can do in their free time.

Group Size

4 or more

Materials

➲ 1 deck of playing cards

Description

Teach the group a card game that you know (the game of Speed is the next game in this chapter and it can be used as the game). Allow the group to play at least one hand of the game.

After teaching the game, ask the group if anyone knows of a different card game they can teach the group. Allow time for the group to play at least one hand of each new game before allowing someone else to teach the group another game. If there is extra time at the end, allow the group to choose their favorite new card game and play it. Allow time to discuss the benefits of learning new activities.

Discussion Prompts

1. Did you learn any new games today that you had never played before?
2. Do you ever feel bored at home and feel that you want to do something new?
3. What are some ways to learn a new activity?
4. What benefit would it be for you to learn new activities?
5. How comfortable did you feel teaching the group a game?
6. Are there any talents or skills you have that you can teach others?

Speed

Objective
To play a fast-paced card game that requires complete focus without getting distracted by everything going on around you.

Who
People who are easily distracted and have trouble staying on task.

Group Size
2 or more

Materials
- ➲ 1 deck of cards for every two players (or use less and have some people take turns).
- ➲ A copy of the *Speed Rules*

Description
　　Play the card game called "Speed" (rules follow) in groups of two. This can be done in a tournament style where winners play winners or where everyone plays everyone and tries to earn points.

Speed Rules
- Two players sit facing each other.
- Deal out five cards face down in one pile between the two players and another pile of five about two feet to the side of the first pile. Place two cards face down and side by side in the middle of the two piles of five.
- Divide the remaining 40 cards between the two players.
- Each player has a pile of 20 cards face down in front of him or her. They should take the top five cards and hold them in their hands.
- On the "go," each player turns over one of the two individual cards that are face down in the middle.
- A player may play any card that is one number up or down

from one of the two cards that is facing up (e.g., if a 3 is facing up, a player can play a 2 or 4 of any suit).

- As soon as a player plays a card, he or she can replace that card with one from his or her own pile. (Each player can have only five cards at a time in his or her hand.)
- At some point, you may find that neither player can make a play from the five cards in their hand. In that case, each one turns over one from the two outside piles and places it in the middle to start the next round.
- The first player to run out of cards wins!

Discussion Prompts

1. Was it easy or difficult for you to focus on this game?
2. What happened if you got distracted and weren't focused?
3. In life, do you find yourself having trouble focusing ever? When?
4. How can you maintain your focus when you need to do so?
5. Did you feel anxiety or pressure to win?
6. How does your body feel when you feel anxious?
7. Do you like competition? Why or why not?

Variation

⮩ Use another high-paced card game that requires people to focus in place of Speed.

Deck of Chance

Objective

For individuals to determine if engaging in a fitness activity has an effect on how they feel emotionally. To encourage people to engage in exercise to improve their own mental and physical health.

Who

People who could benefit from incorporating exercise into their life to improve their fitness level, self-esteem, and emotional well-being.

Group Size

2 or more

Materials

- 2 decks of playing cards
- A copy of the *Exercise List* (Found on page 226 with the *Physical Puzzle* game)

Description

Shuffle one deck of playing cards, and deal one card to each person (for smaller groups you may deal out more than one card to each person). Call out a specific exercise (see the list of ideas on page 226), and select a card from a second deck to determine which individual will have the opportunity to earn points by doing the exercise (the individual who has the matching card in their hand). Alternately, you could call out everyone who has a certain type of card (a club, diamond, heart, spade, even numbered card, odd numbered card, face card, numbered card, red card, black card, etc.) as those that get the chance to earn points by completing the exercise.

Discussion Prompts

1. How can exercising regularly benefit you emotionally?
2. How can improving your fitness level benefit you?
3. What are some ways you like to work out?
4. How often do you work out?
5. What can you do to add more exercise to your daily routine?

Variations

- Check in with everyone before the activity to find out how they're feeling emotionally and physically. Do the same after exercising to compare the difference. Encourage people to use exercise as a coping skill if they feel better after working out.
- Do this activity in a gym or outdoors with exercises such as jumping rope, shooting baskets, running one lap, etc. Do several rounds of this game with new activities announced for each round.
- Set up various stations around the room. Assign different cards to different stations, and have everyone assigned to that station do the activity together.

Going Fishing

Objective
For individuals to determine if engaging in a fitness activity has an effect on how they feel emotionally. To encourage people to engage in exercise to improve their own mental and physical health.

Who
People who could benefit from incorporating exercise into their life to improve their fitness level, self-esteem, and emotional well-being.

Group Size
2 to 6 (This game can also be done with larger groups if you use more than one deck of cards and place the participants in smaller groups.)

Materials
- 1 deck of playing cards for every four people
- A copy of the *Exercise List* (Found on page 226 with the *Physical Puzzle* game)
- Instructions for the classic card game "Go Fish"

Description
Use one deck of playing cards that are shuffled. Announce various exercises (see page 226 for ideas) that individuals may do in order to draw a card from the pile. After each exercise is complete, everyone who did it takes one card from the deck for their hand. Lead the participants in at least eight different exercises so everyone has the opportunity to earn up to eight playing cards.

After the exercise time is complete, allow the group to play a game of "Go Fish" using the playing cards they have in their hand. (Go Fish is a classic card game; rules can be found on the Internet.) Any cards remaining stay in the "Go Fish" pile for the game.

Discussion Prompts

1. Did you earn all eight cards? If not, why didn't you?
2. How often do you get exercise?
3. How can exercising regularly benefit you emotionally?
4. How can improving your fitness level benefit you?
5. What are some ways you like to work out?
6. What can you do to add more exercise to your daily routine?

Variations

➲ Play a game of "Go Fish" by dealing out five cards to each player. Any time a person must draw from the "Go Fish" pile, they have to do an exercise prior to selecting the card. You may have them select the exercise from a list or the person who told them to "Go Fish" selects the exercise.

➲ Play a different card game other than Go Fish after the cards are given out.

Lucky Number

Objective
To increase group interaction, improve social skills, strengthen communication skills, and help people learn more about one another in a non-threatening manner.

Who
People who have difficulty sharing their thoughts and feelings with others.

Group Size
8 or more

Materials
- 1 Die
- 4 sheets of paper
- Marker
- A copy of the *Lucky Number Choices*

Description
In a large room or gym, mark off each corner with a number one, two, three, or four. Gather the group together in the middle of the room, and read one of the sets of choices. Ask people to go to the corner that best represents them. Once there, they may talk about why they chose that corner with the others who are also in that corner.

With everyone in their corner, roll the die (if you roll a 5 or 6, roll again). Whatever number it lands on is the "lucky number." Everyone in that corner earns a point (you may give out pennies, stickers, marbles, or other items to help them keep track of points). You may also do an "unlucky number," where that corner doesn't get a point while those in the other three do. Do several rounds of this before coming together for group discussion time.

Discussion Prompts

1. Do you feel that you know yourself very well, and therefore found it easy to select a corner? Or was it difficult to figure out who you really are?
2. What did you learn about someone else in the group that you didn't already know?
3. Was it easier to talk about yourself in a game like this because the topics give you a way to describe yourself?

Variation

➲ Instead of giving out points, eliminate people who are in an "unlucky" corner until you have one winner at the end.

Lucky Number Choices

1. Are you most like… summer, winter, spring, or fall?
2. Would you most likely be found watching… the news, sports, a "reality" TV show, or a documentary?
3. On a day off, would you most likely be found… playing video games, playing on a sports team, doing chores, or shopping?
4. Are you more like a… potato, banana, bowl of spaghetti, or piece of bread?
5. Would you most likely be found in… sandals, bare feet, boots, or tennis shoes?
6. Where would you most like to go on vacation… tropical island, ski resort, amusement park, or campground?
7. Would you most likely listen to… country music, rock-'n'-roll, classical, or rap?
8. Would you most likely be found eating lunch… alone, with a group of friends, on the go, or skipping lunch altogether?
9. How would you describe your personality… outgoing, shy, both shy and outgoing (depending on the group), in the middle of shy and outgoing?
10. How would you describe your future… exciting, scary, same as today, road to nowhere?

Roll and Move

Objective
To engage in a fast-paced competitive game to encourage exercise and to practice using self-control when in a competitive situation.

Who
People who could benefit from understanding how putting exercise into their routine can benefit them emotionally and physically. People who have a difficult time engaging in competitive activities and could benefit from practicing being in a competitive situation.

Group Size
8 or more

Materials
- ➲ 1 pair of dice for every eight people
- ➲ A copy of the *Roll and Move List*

Description
Divide the group into teams of four to eight participants each. Have each team sit together in a circle. Give every team a pair of dice and the *Roll and Move List*. Let them know the time limit of the activity. When you say "go," one person on each team rolls the dice and does the activity associated with that number from the list. After completing the activity, they must pick up the dice and hand them to the next person. That person then rolls the dice to see what activity it is that he or she must do. Each team should keep track of how many activities they complete before the time limit is up. The team who has completed the most is declared the winner.

Discussion Prompts
1. How were you feeling emotionally and physically before we started this activity?
2. How do you feel emotionally and physically now?

3. How often do you get exercise?
4. How can exercising regularly benefit you emotionally?
5. How can improving your fitness level benefit you?
6. What are some ways you like to work out?
7. What can you do to add more exercise to your daily routine?
8. Did the competitive nature of this game make it more or less fun for you to play?
9. Do you find competition to be a healthy thing for you to engage in? Why or why not?

Variations

⮊ Adjust the list to fit the room you're in. Or do this in the gym, and the group sits in a circle and then does tasks around the gym, such as making two baskets, jumping rope five times, etc.

⮊ Create a list of activities that everyone must do as a group.

Roll and Move List

Roll a…

2 = Do three push-ups.

3 = Do five sit-ups.

4 = Do fifteen jumping jacks.

5 = Give each person on your team a "high five."

6 = March around the room while singing the alphabet.

7 = Run around each of the other teams one time.

8 = Spin around eight times while hopping on one leg.

9 = Jump as high as you can ten times.

10 = Do ten frog hops. (Hop like a frog in place.)

11 = Do a crazy dance for the count of 20.

12 = FREE PASS: you don't have to do anything!

Roll and Run

Objective
To recognize the advantages or disadvantages each person is born with based on the talents, gifts, and challenges they naturally have.

Who
People who always wish they were like someone else, rather than taking the time to recognize the unique qualities they have to offer.

Group Size
8 or more

Materials
- 1 pair of dice for every team (four to eight on each team)
- 1 chair (or other object for the group to run around) for every team

Description
Divide the group into teams of four or more. Give each team one pair of dice and have them line up in a single file line. Place a chair a good distance from each team's line. On the "go" signal, the first person in each line rolls his or her dice. He or she then runs down to the chair for the team and circles it the number of times that came up on the dice. The next person in line does the same as soon as their teammate returns to line. The first team to finish is declared the winner. (You may wish to do this more than once, and the first team to win three times is declared the winner.)

Discussion Prompts
1. What happened when you rolled a high number? A low number?
2. The ones who rolled the lowest numbers ended up with an advantage. Was that fair?
3. Have you played a game against someone else and felt that it wasn't fair because the other person or team had an unfair advantage?

4. Have you ever been a part of a team or group where you felt that things were easier for others because they had more of an advantage over you (they were born faster, stronger, with music talent, smarter, etc.)?
5. What talents do you have that others don't have that give you an advantage?
6. How are you using these talents? Are there ways you could better use your talents?
7. Is it OK to recognize the things you're good at doing? Why or why not?
8. Is there someone in this group that has a talent that could give them an advantage in life, however you don't think they recognize it or don't use it fully?

Variations
➲ Use an object other than a chair to run around: a hula hoop on the ground, a pillow, another person, etc.
➲ Use one die instead of a pair of dice.
➲ If at anytime a seven is rolled, that person must take two turns in a row.

One Hundred!

Objective
To discuss the need to use time wisely to finish tasks, such as homework or other undertakings that require people to be self-motivated to get them done.

Who
Individuals who don't use their time wisely and find themselves behind in many areas of their lives.

Group Size
4 or more

Materials
- 1 die for every eight people, plus one extra die
- 1 pen for every eight people
- 1 piece of paper for each person

Description
If you have more than eight people, divide the large group into smaller groups of four to eight and give each group one die. Give every person one piece of scrap paper. Each group should be seated in a circle, either on the floor or at a table, with a pen in the middle. One person from each group hold a die.

The leader has a die and rolls it and then calls out the "magic number" that comes up. The person with the die in each group also rolls it, and if the magic number comes up, he or she can grab the pen and start writing out the numbers 1 through 100 on his or her paper. If the magic number doesn't come up, he or she simply passes the die to the next person who gives it a roll. The die is in constant motion, being passed around the circle. Each time someone rolls the magic number, they gain possession of the pen (the person who was writing must stop and give up the pen). Whenever a person gains possession of the pen, they start where they left off with the numbers. The first person in each group to reach 100 is the winner of that group!

Discussion Prompts

1. When you gained control of the pen and were writing out numbers, how quickly were you writing? Why did you move this quickly?
2. When you didn't have the pen, were you hoping you would roll the magic number so you could get the pen? How did you feel when you were waiting?
3. Do you ever find yourself with just a limited amount of time to get your work done?
4. When you have a block of time to get your work/homework done, how effectively would you say you use your time?
5. If you don't use your time effectively, what are the consequences?
6. What things distract you and keep you from getting your work done?
7. What changes can you make in your life to ensure that you use your time wisely?

Variation

⇨ When one group has a winner, the remaining players continue to play for second place.

Poker Challenge

Objective
For a group of people to use teamwork to accomplish various challenges.

Who
People who need to practice working with others to improve social skills.

Group Size
10 or more

Materials
➲ 1 deck of playing cards
➲ A copy of the *Challenge List* (found on the following page)

Description
Divide the groups into teams of five to ten members each. Announce different challenges that the groups must each try to accomplish as a team (see the *Challenge List*). Give each group a turn to accomplish the challenge, and if they do so, give them one playing card from a shuffled deck of cards. Each team should make sure that no one on the other teams can see their cards at any time.

Go through several challenges, and hand out at least five playing cards to each group. Next, instruct the teams to select their best five cards for a hand of poker. Each team sends up one player to the front with their five cards. Ask one team representative at a time to show their hand to determine who the winner is.

Discussion Prompts
1. Was this game fair? Why or why not?
2. What did your team have to do in order to have a better chance of winning this game? Did your team do this?

3. What does each individual have to do in order for a group to be successful when working together to accomplish a task?
4. In your life, when do you have to work with others as a part of a team?
5. What role do you usually take when in a group? Leader, follower, contributor, etc.?
6. What role would you like to take?
7. What can you do to gain the skills needed to take on that role?

Variation

➲ Give each team the list of challenges and a time limit. For each challenge they accomplish, they get one card, but the teams can do as many as possible during the time limit.

Challenge List

1. Build a pyramid.
2. Sing a commercial.
3. As a team complete 100 total push ups.
4. In pairs, sit on the ground facing each other with your toes touching. Grab hands and pull each other up.
5. Sit in a tight circle with backs together and facing outside the circle with arms linked, then as a group stand up.
6. Your team must leapfrog from the starting point and end at a finish line. (Both the starting point and finish line should be designated by the leader.)
7. A member of your team must say the alphabet backwards from Z to A.
8. As a group, name 15 different holidays, and each person on your team must name at least one.
9. Sing a chorus of a song with the words "truth" or "true" in it.
10. Line up by your shoe size without talking.
11. Everyone together must sing a nursery rhyme.
12. Your team members stand in a circle and face each other. You must go for 20 seconds without anyone laughing.
13. One member of your team must say the Pledge of Allegiance correctly.
14. One person must do a headstand or handstand and hold it for five seconds.
15. Your team must name 24 animals (one animal that starts with each letter of the alphabet, but you can choose two letters to skip).

ACTIVE

This chapter is different from the others in that the games are all active. They can all be played with a handful of foam balls, plus a few other supplies, instead of using a board game. Some groups will benefit from having the opportunity to be active and get some energy out. You won't have to give up the therapeutic experience because the game is active; just be sure to use the Therapeutic Discussion Prompts found with each game.

Over the years, I've lead a lot of active games with various groups. In this chapter, I am including the games that are always the favorites of every group I have worked with. An element of competition is present in these games, and at times, individuals will get "out". But these active games are designed so it's very easy to get back "in" with the help of teammates or by a player's own efforts.

Therapeutic Applications of Active Games

Each game is unique and offers its own Discussion Prompts and Therapeutic Applications. However, the theme of using physical fitness as a means of improving one's life both physically and emotionally can always be used for any active game.

Discussion Prompts: Benefits of exercise

1. How were you feeling emotionally and physically before we started this activity?
2. How do you feel emotionally and physically now?
3. How often do you get exercise?
4. How can exercising regularly benefit you emotionally?
5. How can improving your fitness level benefit you?
6. What are some ways you like to work out?
7. What can you do to add more exercise to your daily routine?

ACTIVE
Games

Bench Ball

Objective

To play a fun active game where individuals are encouraged to cheer against the person who got them "out" to open the door to talking about feelings they may have towards people who they feel have gone against them.

Who

People who focus on how others have "wronged" them, rather than taking control of their own future to make healthy choices.

Group Size

8 to 30 is ideal

Materials

➲ 4 foam balls

Description

   To start this game, scatter the foam balls throughout the play area. Designate the boundaries for the game including an area on the side where everyone who is hit by a ball must go when they are "out".

   On the go signal anyone can pick up any ball that is in the area and take no more than three steps with it before throwing it at another player. When any of the players are hit with the ball they should make sure they know who got them out and then go stand on the sideline. A player who throws a ball that is caught by another player is also out and must go to the sideline and make note of who got them out. All players who are out must watch the game carefully to see when the person who got them out gets out. When a player goes out then all those on the sideline whom that person got out can reenter the game.

   It is fun to encourage kids to cheer for the person who got them out to get out, so they can reenter the game. When several people are cheering for someone to get out it means that person is a strong player and they will like hearing their name chanted by several of the players who are on the sidelines.

Discussion Prompts
1. How did it feel for you to cheer for someone else to get out so you could get back in?
2. Did you like hearing others cheer for you to get out because it meant you had done a good job getting others out?
3. Do you ever wish for someone else to fail because they hurt you and you want to see them hurt? If so, why?
4. Do you ever wish for someone else to fail because they have more than you and you might be jealous?
5. If you ever wish for others to fail do you think this is a healthy thing for you to do?
6. How can you overcome your desire for others to fail?

Variation
➲ This can be played as a soccer or basketball game. Everyone has a ball and must dribble it around the area (soccer style or basketball style) while at the same time trying to knock the ball out of bounds that someone else is dribbling. A player may reenter the game when the person who got them out goes out.

Doctor Ball

Objective
To play a fun, active group game that will lead to a discussion on accepting help from others in order to get back into the "game" of life.

Who
People who try to do everything on their own and who rarely accept help from others.

Group Size
12 to 40 is ideal

Materials
- Several foam balls
- One foam swim noodle cut into fourths (or roll up pieces of paper and tape them closed to create two wands)
- Something that can be used to mark off two small areas (Two gym mats, or two hula hoops, or two ropes, or small cones, etc.)

Description
Divide the group into two equal teams and select one person from each team to be the team doctor. Give each doctor a "healing wand" (a piece of a foam noodle that is about one foot long). Designate an area on each end of the gym (or play area) to be the "hospital" and mark off this area. The two doctors start the game in their respective hospitals where they are safe. Once a doctor leaves their hospital they can get out if hit by a ball.

Divide the balls evenly among the two teams and on the "go" signal players must stay on their own side of the gym but try to get members of the other team out by hitting them with a ball that is thrown. If the ball is caught, then the thrower is the one who is out. Once a player is out they must sit down in the spot where they were hit and wait to be healed by the doctor who must touch them with the healing wand before they can return to the game. The first team to get the other team's doctor out wins the game. At the start of each new round select two new doctors.

Discussion Prompts

1. Did you feel helpless when you were out?
2. How did you feel once you were "healed" and could return to the game?
3. Could you have returned to the game under your own power without waiting for a Doctor to save you?
4. Can you think of a situation in your own life when you have tried to do things without getting any help from others and it was a struggle for you?
5. Are you willing to accept help from others? Why or why not?
6. How could your life improve if you were to accept help that others offer to you?

Protector

Objective
To play a fun active game where people take turns "protecting" their teammates leading to a discussion about what we can do to protect those we love, and what individuals can do to find protection when in difficult situations.

Who
People who often find themselves in situations that are dangerous who need to find a way to get protection in order to avoid getting hurt. People who harm others who need to understand that others need to be protected from their actions.

Group Size
20 to 40 is ideal

Materials
- ➲ Two large (soccer ball size) soft foam balls
- ➲ Small cones, or tape, or rope to mark off two large circles

Description
Mark off two large circles with cones, tape, rope, or other items. Each circle should be ten yards in diameter with about fifteen yards distance between the two circles. Divide the group into two equal teams with one team standing on the outside edge of one of the two circles and the opposing team on the outside of the other circle.

Each team selects five members to send to the middle of the other team's circle and designate one member of that group of five be the "protector". Each team has a ball (the players on the outside of the two circles have the balls) and on the "go" signal tries to get the members of the opposing team (who are in the center of their circle) out by hitting them with the foam ball in the air. The protector cannot get out and this person can block the ball to protect his or her team. If a protector catches the ball he or she must toss it back to a member of the other team. Once a player is hit and they are out they can return to their own circle and help in getting the other team out.

The first team to get all four members of the opposing team out wins the round. After each round select a new group to go into the middle of the other team's circle.

Discussion Prompts

1. Which role did you like the best? Protector, Protected, or trying to get the other team out? Why?
2. Which of these roles do you identify with the most? Are you always trying to protect someone else? Are you in need of protection from others? Are you trying to harm someone who may need protection from you?
3. How can you improve the situation you find yourself in?

Variation

➲ For larger groups you may wish to send more than five members to the opposing circle.

Capture

Objective
To play a high energy active game to focus on the benefits of engaging in a fitness activity to ensure a healthy balanced lifestyle.

Who
People who need to think about incorporating fitness into their daily routine to improve their emotional and physical state.

Group Size
20 to 40 is ideal

Materials
- Items that can me used to mark of two squares (8 small cones work well)
- 8 foam balls (or use bandanas or other similar items)

Description
Divide the group into two teams with one team on each half of the gym. Use the cones to make a box about fifteen feet long and five feet deep on each side, equal distance from the center line (about thirty feet back is good). Place four balls inside each box. The object of the game is to capture all eight balls before the other team does using the following rules to play:

1. Both teams are safe on their own side of the gym but once a player crosses the center line into the other team's territory they can be tagged.
2. When a player is tagged they must sit down in that spot and cannot be freed until their own teammate crosses the line and tags them.
3. Once a teammate has tagged someone who is sitting they both get free backs to go back to their side and they have to go back before trying to capture one of the balls.

4. If a player makes it into the box containing the balls they are in a safe zone, and cannot be tagged until they come out of the box. The defending team may not go into the box.
5. Any ball taken out of the other team's box and carried across the center line without the person carrying it being tagged is successfully captured.
6. If a person who is carrying a ball is tagged that ball goes back into the box where it came from.
7. Only one ball can be captured at a time.
8. All captured balls are placed inside the box of the team that captured it, the first team to capture all eight balls wins the game.

This is one of those games that can go back and forth for quite a while and can easily be called as a tie if the leader waits until both teams are back to four balls a piece.

Discussion Prompts
1. Did you have fun?
2. How often do you engage in fitness activities?
3. Do you find it easier to workout when engaged in a competitive game than you do when just running or working out? Why or why not?
4. How can you increase the amount of exercise you engage in?
5. How can you use exercise as a coping skill or alternative to unhealthy behavior?

Variation
➲ Mark off an additional box on each side that is the jail. When a player is tagged they must go to jail. All the members of a team that are in a jail can be freed if a member of their own team tosses a ball and one of the people in jail catches the ball. However that ball must then go to the other team as a captured ball. If a ball is thrown and nobody catches it then the ball goes to the other team but everyone remains in jail.

Magic Wands

Objective
To play a fun, active group game that will lead to a discussion on being a part of a group where individuals can offer help to each other when a member of the group needs help. This can also be used as a fun fitness activity.

Who
People who struggle with accepting help from others.

Group Size
20 to 40 is ideal

Materials
- A pile of foam balls
- 8 magic wands (roll up pieces of paper and tape them closed to create a wand)

Description
Divide the group into two teams and separate the two teams with one team on each half of the gym. Give each team four of the magic wands. Each team must select four different players to hold onto the magic wands. The wands are used to get players back into the game who have gotten out.

The game is played by both teams throwing balls across the center line to try and hit each other and get players from the other team out. When hit by a ball the player who is hit must sit down in the spot they were hit and wait for a person with a magic wand to touch them with the wand to get him back into the game. (If a ball is thrown and caught by a player from the opposite team the player who threw the ball is out and must sit down). If a player who has a magic wand becomes out they must sit down and give up their magic wand to the leader and no longer have magical powers. The first team to get the opposing team to give up all of their magical wands wins the game. Start the next round by selecting new people to give the magical objects too.

Discussion Prompts

1. Did you feel helpless when you were out?
2. How did you feel once you were "healed" and could return to the game?
3. Could you have returned to the game under your own power without waiting for a healer to save you?
4. Can you think of a situation in your own life when you have tried to do things without getting any help from others and it was a struggle for you?
5. Are you willing to accept help from others? Why or why not?
6. How can you learn from others who are a part of this group and how can they help you?
7. How could your life improve if you were to accept help that others offer to you?

Get Back Up!

Objective
To compare the difference between engaging in activity as an individual versus as a part of a team

Who
People who could benefit from learning about the benefits of working together with others as a part of a team.

Group Size
10-25 is ideal

Materials
➲ 2 large (soccer ball size) foam balls

Description
   Designate the boundaries of the play area and toss the two balls out. The first two people to grab either of the balls can take three steps with it and throw it to try to get anyone else out by hitting them with the ball (without the ball touching the ground first). If a ball is caught then the thrower is out. Once a ball is thrown and loose anyone else can grab it and attempt to get any member of the group out. When a player is hit by the ball he or she must sit down in the spot where they were hit but can reenter the game by grabbing a loose ball as it rolls past them and from the sitting position throw it and get someone who is standing out so they can stand up and reenter the game. When just one or two people remain standing declare them the winner/s.
   For the second round designate two teams (it is easiest to break the groups into two easily identifiable teams - boys versus girls or people wearing pants versus people wearing shorts, etc.). Team members try to work together to get all the members of the opposite team out before their own team is all seated. Team members can pass the ball to each other and help those who are sitting to get back up.

Discussion Prompts

1. Did you enjoy playing in teams or as individuals more? Why?
2. Did you feel powerless to get back into the game when you were playing as an individual?
3. Did you feel you had more opportunity to get back in the game when you had teammates who could help you?
4. Do you tend to try and do everything by yourself or do you rely on others to help you? Which is better?
5. Do you have a support group in your life you can call on for help when you need it?
6. If you would like to have a team of people you could rely on to help you out how can you find a support group like this?

Resources

TABOO is a trademark of Hersch and Company. JENGA is a trademark of Pokonobe Associates and is manufactured under license from Hasbro. SCRABBLE is a trademark of Hasbro in the US and Canada. MONOPOLY, OPERATION, CHUTES AND LADDERS are trademarks of Hasbro. © 2013 Hasbro. All Rights Reserved. Used with permission.

APPLES TO APPLES and associated trademarks and trade dress are owned by, and used under permission from, Mattel, Inc. ©2013 Mattel, Inc. All Rights Reserved.

IMAGINIFF and associated trademarks and trade dress are owned by, and used under permission from, Mattel, Inc. ©2013 Mattel, Inc. All Rights Reserved.

RORY'S STORY CUBES is a registered trademark of The Creativity Hub Ltd. ©2013 Gamewright, a division of Ceaco. Used with permission.

BANANAGRAMS is a registered trademark of Banangrams. ©2013 Bananagrams. Used with permission.

LET'S GO FISHIN' is a registered trademark of Pressman Toy Corporation. ©2013 Pressman Toy Corporation. Used with permission.

THE UNGAME is a registered trademark of Talicor Inc. ©2013 Talicor, Inc. Used without permission.

Index of Therapeutic Topics covered in each game

(Cope - Coping Skills, SD - Self-Discovery, SE - Self-Esteem, Comm - Communication Skills, AM - Anger Management, T - Teamwork)

If you liked this book you will enjoy these
other titles by Alanna Jones.

104 Activities that Build: Self-Esteem, Teamwork, Communication, Anger Management, Self-Discovery, and Coping Skills

Team-Building Activities for Every Group

More Team-Building Activities for Every Group

The wRECking Yard of Games and Activities

Fun and Active Group Games! Exciting gym and outdoor games for physical education classes, youth groups, camps, and clubs.

Fun Soccer Drills that Teach Soccer Skills to 5, 6, and 7 year olds

For more information and to find free sample
games from all these books go to
www.gamesforgroups.com